Jesus
is Enough!

One church's transformation from spiritual
consumers to more mature followers of Christ

*A devotional journey through the Scriptures, designed to
restore true joy through the person and work of Christ
and His gospel, and encourage Christians to seek the
Master rather than what's on the Master's table.*

Dr. Carlton C. McLeod

WestBow
PRESS
A DIVISION OF THOMAS NELSON

Unless otherwise indicated, all Scripture quotations are from The Holy Bible, English Standard Version®,
copyright © 2001 by Crossway Bibles, a publishing ministry of Good News Publishers. Used by permission.
All rights reserved." Italics and/or underlines added to ESV quotations indicate the author's emphasis.

Scripture quotations marked (The Message) are taken from The Message. Copyright © 1993,
1994, 1995, 1996, 2000, 2001, 2002. Used by permission of NavPress Publishing Group.

Scripture quotations marked (NIV) are taken from The Holy Bible, New International Version®,
NIV® Copyright © 1973, 1978, 1984, 2011 by International Bible Society. Used by permission.

WestBow Press books may be ordered through booksellers or by contacting:

WestBow Press
A Division of Thomas Nelson
1663 Liberty Drive
Bloomington, IN 47403
www.westbowpress.com
1 (866) 928-1240

Because of the dynamic nature of the Internet, any web addresses or links contained in
this book may have changed since publication and may no longer be valid. The views
expressed in this work are solely those of the author and do not necessarily reflect the views
of the publisher, and the publisher hereby disclaims any responsibility for them.

Any people depicted in stock imagery provided by Thinkstock are models,
and such images are being used for illustrative purposes only.
Certain stock imagery © Thinkstock.

ISBN: 978-1-4908-1806-1 (sc)
ISBN: 978-1-4908-1805-4 (e)

Library of Congress Control Number: 2013922043

Printed in the United States of America.

WestBow Press rev. date: 1/15/2014

To Donna, my wife, my queen, and my best friend,
who has taken every step of this ministry journey with me
with joy, beauty, and a deep, abiding love for Christ.

CONTENTS

PREFACE

The year is 2007 ... I'm frustrated. Very frustrated. I had been the senior pastor of Calvary Revival Church Chesapeake (CRCC, formally Closer Walk Christian Fellowship) for ten years at that point. The church averaged over four hundred people in attendance. We had a small but adequate building. The church was growing, and we had money in the bank. Sounds good right? So what's up with all the frustration?

Well, at the time, I jokingly called it my "mid-ministry crisis!" To give you an idea of how I was feeling, here is a personal devotional I wrote as I was working through my feelings back then. I ominously called it The Black Box:

The Black Box

(A lament for African-American pastors wanting to move beyond the box!)

Why must I preach, teach, and lead like other pastors? Why is the media model I see constantly my standard? Why can't I be free to reach out to people in the way God has given me? What am I afraid of?

1. I'm afraid to face my own views of success and validation. If I don't build what everyone else builds (and do it better than they do), I'll struggle with feeling "successful."
2. I'm afraid to go against the status quo. It is truly amazing that our non-tradition is now tradition.
3. I'm afraid of what other preachers will say. "Where is his building?" "He told them not to give so much?" "I thought he would be the next [*insert high-profile name here*]."
4. I'm afraid to differ from my mentor's model even though I think he would let me be me.
5. I'm afraid that my own people won't understand and/or put up with how different we really are for a "black church." African-Americans, in particular, are used to a certain ministry model.

The question is, "*Will I let this prevent me from walking in the vision God has given me?*"

The current "successful black church" ministry model:

1. Preaching that focuses on taking people to their own next level and breakthrough
2. Nice buildings and the fundraising that goes with them
3. A focus on the big gathering
4. Personal marketing (i.e., books, cds, television, etc.)
5. Conferences and guest speaking, which I find exhausting. Is it wrong to rather be at a movie with friends and family?
6. The key man model; ministry built around the senior pastor's preaching
7. Titles and personal support staff for "the man"

With as much honesty as I can muster, what has God put in my heart for now?

1. I don't care about buildings, I care about people, and I certainly don't want the bondage of a corporate mortgage. There is a need for the corporate gathering, but I'd rather see people use extra money to get out of personal debt than "build me a church." I have no desire to buy land and build.
2. I feel called to apostolic ministry. I want to plant bible based churches and serve pastors.
3. I want to reach both hip hop culture and pop culture. I want to reach all races and socio-economic brackets.
4. I don't care about how big I get. I'm quickly getting over needing to gather a large audience to feel successful.
5. I have no desire to preach at or host conferences. I'd rather preach in small churches or to groups of leaders.
6. I want to use technology to keep people connected.
7. I want to see young black men embrace integrity, learning, and, of course, Christ.

Where does all this leave me? Will I be true to me or will I cave under the pressure to conform?

Now having the perspective of six additional years, when I began to pursue God's calling and moved away from the "successful model," God gave me some of that stuff anyway! As of this writing we are in a debt-free building, overseeing pastors, planning conferences on integrity rather than getting stuff, pushing an old but powerful vision called the D6Reformation (see D6Reformation.org) and somehow, the church has still grown! God indeed has a sense of humor! Anyway, on with the story …

A Good Decision

Well, after all this consternation, I did decide (by God's grace) to open up my mind and heart to the leading of the Spirit and to an expository look at the New Testament. This book chronicles that journey.

And I must tell you … it was hard! I had no idea that I would face such opposition to the gospel—by Christians no less! I also didn't realize how much Christians tie their joy and peace to the ups and downs of the world. For people who have been commanded, "Do not love the world or the things in the world" (1 John 2:15), we sure do love us some world!

So in about a year and a half, we systematically worked our way through three epistles of Paul, and God really began to open our eyes. He exposed how we had traded in a biblical view of the gospel for a worldly, Wall Street sort of view, where God is obligated to give us what we want. Many good books have been written on this subject, including *The Gospel According to Jesus*[1] and *Hard to Believe*[2] by John MacArthur and *Christianity in Crisis*[3] by Hank Hanegraaff. However, my hope is that you can appreciate our own journey as a church. This book is designed to walk you line by line through the Scriptures and take you on our own journey to the inescapable and wonderful conclusion that *Jesus is enough!*

Jesus Is Enough!

Many believers struggle to find meaning and fulfillment. They navigate the waters of life searching desperately for joy and peace. These believers desire to be successful in life but do not feel like they have achieved anything. They are told that if they just wait long enough, a powerful blessing or breakthrough will come, and their desires will be fulfilled. "When will Christ manifest this blessing?" they wonder. "Where has Christ gone?" Christ hasn't gone anywhere! He's just been overshadowed by what I jokingly call, "Systematic Blessing Theology!" Our inability to understand the simple truths of the Gospel and our desire to bring business models into the church have also reduced our reliance on Christ.

I mean, sometimes I had to ask myself, *Has the church lost its mind?* Why are we telling people to focus so much on things that fade away? Now, if some of those things come as a result of contentment and hard work, wonderful! Ultimately people should be taught that they come as a result of Christ's cross! He died to pay the penalty for our sin, not so we can "win" in life!

Jesus is enough to have joy! *Jesus is enough* to walk in peace and contentment! In Jesus, you can feel successful in life. Simply being faithful to Him and His commands *is* success! *Jesus is enough* during the difficult times! *Jesus is enough* to experience "breakthrough" because He is the breakthrough! *Jesus is enough* to adjust our perspective, freeing us daily from the temporary, temporal confines of this earth to live with eternal and unchanging realities.

For the Sake of Clarity

Now, to make sure I don't give the impression that CRCC was a full-blown, card-carrying, "come get your blessing" kind of church, let me honestly say that I have never fully ascribed to the prosperity gospel. I never had any one thousand dollar miracle lines. I never dreamed up a completely arbitrary offering by wrenching an Old Testament festival completely out of context. I never offered Christ as the key to someone's Lexus (after suitable naming and claiming of course)! But I did teach for years and years that Christ was the key to circumstantial happiness. For example, "Just do these three things and everything will work out"—that kind of stuff. Not heretical by any means, but certainly not "gospel" either. I subtly offered Christ as a leadership coach and marriage counselor as opposed to King of Kings and Lord of Lords! Christ does teach us how to lead better and help our families and marriages become stronger. However, God shifted us from pursuing Christ purely for those things to seeking Christ because He is Christ!

A Word about Expository Preaching

I can also say that this journey was solidified and strengthened through expository preaching. Most Bible expositors strongly recommended expository preaching, but for some reason I rarely used the method in favor of topical, "practical" lessons. Once I started though, the truth that Jesus is enough was easily apparent. Expository preaching forces the preacher to examine the context more carefully, consider both the author and the audience, ask the right hermeneutical questions, and limit personal presuppositions and cultural biases. In short, the Holy Spirit led us to take God at His Word line by line, and when He did, the truth of Christ and His gospel took center stage as opposed to the desires of the preacher to please the flock. As we went through this journey, we spent some initial time in Matthew and then walked line by line through Philippians, Colossians, and most of Ephesians. As you'll see, I improved as an exegete as I went along!

So do this: look around for churches that practice expository preaching and look at the message that consequently comes out. It is very difficult to find a church moving line-by-line through large swaths of Scripture that also paints Christ as a self-help guru or the key to personal success. It just doesn't happen. On the other hand, the topical method seems to foster this mind-set quite often. I believe that when the church became self-help centers instead of "pillars of truth," American Christianity lost its soul and its strength.

How to Use this Book

What follows is our journey, one that took our church a year and a half. This book is composed of sermons and leadership lessons we preached as the Lord shaped us and molded us into a more mature body of believers. I have organized it in a way that allows you to see our process of discovery as we pressed through the riches of God's Word. The lessons will give you an opportunity to apply them to your life as well. As I looked back, I also added some personal thoughts about both the price we paid and the blessing we experienced as we relentlessly refocused on Christ.

This book is designed to be used with your Bible. In fact, you'll miss the essence of *Jesus is Enough* if you just read the book without reading your Bible. Read the Scripture text, the lesson, and take anywhere from one full day up to a week per lesson. Make sure you discuss your insights with your family, friends, or small group, and write out your thoughts about how He is becoming truly enough for you.

Lastly, when you read the Scriptures, do so with these solid and time-tested interpretive rules noted by authors Gordon Fee and Douglas Stewart in *How to Read the Bible for all its worth*:

Rule 1: A text cannot mean what it never could have meant to its author or his or her hearers.

This rule anchors us into the author's and hearer's context and gives us a "foundation" from which to interpret and apply the passage we are reading.

Rule 2: Whenever we share the same context with the original hearers, God's Word to us is the same as His Word to them.

Christian Research Institute's President, Hank Hanegraaff, coined the acronym L-I-G-H-T-S to help us remember how to begin with solid interpretation. The acronym stands for Literal principle, Illumination by the Holy Spirit, Grammatical construction, Historical setting, Typology (especially in the Old Testament), and scriptural synergy (seeing how all Scripture works together). While we do not have time to review them here, it should be noted that biblical context should be understood as well. Think of it as C-L-I-G-H-T-S. Understanding the context of a text will help to point the reader in the right direction.

Rule 3: The clear must interpret the unclear.

Here is the process: Keeping all the rules in mind, we start with biblical commands. Then we move to principles and finally to patterns—*in that order*. In the absence of one, we move to the next. Commands inform principles and supersede patterns. The patterns themselves must be considered in light of both commands and principles. *When we have a command in context, we have God's Word on an issue and other passages must be interpreted in light of what is clearly stated.* This is a *huge* point.

In November of 2013, I had the opportunity to speak with Harvey Bluedorn, a noted author on a variety of subjects including the Greek language, logic, and Christian classical education in homeschooling. We were discussing how to interpret unclear passages and he explained it this way: *"The clear should shed light upon the unclear or obscure—not the other way around."* Bluedorn explained that our tendency is to take an unclear passage and use it to invalidate a "contrary" teaching found in clear passages that directly teach on the subject. "To put the obscure passage in control," says Bluedorn "is to stand all methods of understanding on their head."

In the absence of commands, we then look to principles, and we do so considering those principles that are overarching. These include God's power (His sovereignty), God's person (His character), and God's plan. This also includes viewing passages through the lens of Christ; His person, His gospel, His work, and His new covenant. This is especially helpful in understanding the Old Testament.

The apostle Paul wrote, "To live is Christ; to die is gain" (Phil. 1:21). Amen and amen. May this book teach you that simple truth, and may it transform your life.

Soli Deo Gloria!
Carlton C. McLeod

BEFORE WE BEGIN ... PREACH THE WORD!

On May 6, 2007, I read 2 Timothy 4:1–5 and said the following words to my church. In my mind and heart, I had drawn a scary line in the sand. I had determined to allow the Lord to take control of the ministry and shape it any way He chose. But I was nervous, on edge, and, well ... afraid! Afraid of what? Change! What would they say? How would they respond? Was I about to kill my church?

> "I charge you in the presence of God and of Christ Jesus, who is to judge the living and the dead, and by his appearing and his kingdom: preach the word; be ready in season and out of season; reprove, rebuke, and exhort, with complete patience and teaching. For the time is coming when people will not endure sound teaching, but having itching ears they will accumulate for themselves teachers to suit their own passions, and will turn away from listening to the truth and wander off into myths. As for you, always be sober-minded, endure suffering, do the work of an evangelist, fulfill your ministry" (2 Tim. 4:1–5).

> Today, my friends, this Scripture has my heart beating fast. In the interest of transparency, I want you to know where I am as a pastor and teacher right now. Up to this point, my ministry has been focused on practical, topical teaching and ministering to the felt needs of those that come to CRCC. I will continue to do this, as it is a part of our calling.

> However, I feel the Lord shifting us a bit, as if His desire is to move us away from searching the Word for a blessing to searching the Word for the blessor. In other words, instead of coming to church to "fix my marriage," we should come to church to fixate on the Master. Honestly, the other method has left me (and many of you) thirsty.

> Christ is calling us to maturity, to be fully formed, loving Him for His sake, not ours. Paul said, "I also count all things loss for the excellence of the

knowledge of Christ Jesus my Lord, for whom I have suffered the loss of all things, and count them as rubbish, that I may gain Christ." Then he went on to say, "Therefore let us, as many as are mature, have this mind" (Phil. 3:8, 15).

I'm now convinced that in order for us to move into the place where God wants us to be, each of us must deepen our relationship with Christ. Our motives (and subsequently our motions) must become more pure. We must resist our consumer impulses and embrace a more New Testament understanding of what it means to be a Christian.

These words marked the beginning of an almost two-year journey that revived my passion for the Word, reframed our corporate understanding of Christ and His gospel, and restored (in my opinion) a more holy walk for our church that lined up with the pathway of God. From then until now, we have pursued Christ relentlessly and doggedly throughout the whole of Scripture. We have looked with loving but biblically critical eyes at *everything*, from church structure and polity to worship practices and evangelism. We even looked biblically at how and through what process a person is saved.

And you know what? It has been simply wonderful! I wouldn't trade anything for the view of Christ we have now. Through any and every trial and good time, He has become enough. In fact, He is more than enough! I'm so glad I endured the fear and stepped out of the boat of Christian normalcy to search harder for Christ. Are you ready to do the same?

Jesus Is Enough **Questions:** Can you learn anything from my fear in the context of Christ? What did I risk when I made this shift in congregant-centered messages to God-centered messages? Have you ever been in a similar situation? What did you do?

_____

_____

_____

_____

_____

_____

_____

_____

_____

_____

_____

_____

REDEFINING BLESSINGS!

Here we go! No more Systematic Blessing Theology, which means the preaching of every single Scripture as a pathway to one's new house, car, lucrative business venture, or personal miracle. Scriptures deemed too hard to fit into this blessing theology are simply ignored. The sad truth is that when Christianity is redefined as a "come get what you want" faith, it actually hurts us, the believers, who become just as susceptible to the emotional blessing roller coaster as the world. We begin trying to control our circumstances with our faith. In the end, we commit idolatry, as our faith becomes sovereign instead of God.

Read Mathew 5:1–12

In His first extended sermon (known as the Sermon on the Mount), Jesus begins a process of developing us to be more like Him. As you will see, His emphasis is on heart transformation and holiness. You'll also find that His definition of blessings may be different from ours. *Blessings are not what you get but who you are.* Ultimately, the greatest blessing is Christ and our learning to be like Him. We must return to the place where Jesus is enough and He becomes our ultimate definition of success.

Thoughts from the text:

1. Blessings flow from your dependency upon Jesus (v. 3).

    It is easy for man to claim that he is dependent only on himself. It is part of our nature to desire to be in complete control. This desire is also a result of a fallen world. To be "poor in spirit" is to realize that you are not self-sufficient and never will be. The kingdom of heaven belongs to those who put their complete trust in the Lord. Again, this isn't something we do naturally. It requires a dying of self, which is a key goal in the Christian walk. When we think of how many books, programs, and sermons are preached on how we can get this or that or how we can find fulfillment (I've preached my share of them), we realize that we've missed a key truth. What we are looking for is not found in us. It is found in Him.

2. Blessings flow from brokenness (v. 4).

Psalm 51:17 states, "The sacrifices of God are a broken spirit; a broken and contrite heart, O God, you will not despise." Furthermore, Isaiah 66:1–2 indicate that God created all things. He needs nothing from us. Yet God focuses His attention on the person "who is humble and contrite in spirit and trembles at [His] word." We must return to the place where sin breaks us and we mourn sinful activity. When was the last time you were truly broken over your own sin and the sins of this nation?

3. Blessings flow from contentment and self-control (v. 5).

Godly contentment and self-control both mean that no matter what God chooses to do, we will be meek toward God and accept all His decisions as good. Far from weakness, meekness is strength under control. It is not self-assertiveness or self-interest. Instead, meekness is a total reliance on God. It is not an act of man but the work of the Holy Spirit. I like the way *The Message* Bible states this verse: "You're blessed when you're content with just who you are—no more, no less. That's the moment you find yourselves proud owners of everything that can't be bought."

4. Blessings flow from simple, right living (v. 6).

Now be honest. Do you really hunger to do what is right? If not, why not? What needs to change to get you to that place? "You're blessed when you've worked up a good appetite for God. He's food and drink in the best meal you'll ever eat" (MSG). You can never go wrong chasing after righteousness. It is our primary duty as Christians. Matthew 6:33 tells us to seek the kingdom of God "and his righteousness" before all other things. In short, live right and God will bless.

5. Blessings flow from true, godly compassion (v. 7).

Mercy can be defined as having compassion or kind forbearance toward another person. Luke tells us to be merciful even as God is merciful. As Christians, we view ourselves as products of God's mercy, which is a communicable attribute that God has elected to share with us. The Lord blesses us when we show compassion for others. "You're blessed when you care. At the moment of being 'careful,' you find yourselves cared for" (MSG).

6. Blessings flow from a heart that loves Jesus (v. 8).

Again, *The Message* Bible articulates this well: "You're blessed when you get your inside world—your mind and heart—put right. Then you can see God in the outside world." Jesus is the definition of purity, so biblical purity cannot exist apart from loving Christ. *Please get this: What you hunger for is available right now! Circumstances do not dictate success! Allow the Holy Spirit to shift your heart from consumer to Christ; everything around you will look different!*

7. Blessings flow from unity (v. 9).

There is nothing worse than division. Through unity, God's children are blessed. Be a son or daughter of God. Paul teaches us in Ephesians to walk in a way that is worthy of our calling with humility and gentleness. We should be eager to maintain the unity of one body and one Spirit. "You're blessed when you can show people how to cooperate instead of compete or fight. That's when you discover who you really are, and your place in God's family" (MSG). Work to bring people together under the banner of Christ.

8. Blessings flow from how you handle hard times (v. 10).

"You're blessed when your commitment to God provokes persecution. The persecution drives you even deeper into God's kingdom" (MSG). Did Jesus really say this? Yes, He did! I know we don't like this one, but it is still true. Sometimes pain is God's megaphone. God loves to turn our pain into purpose. Just as He was glorified by the death of New Testament saints, He is glorified by our conforming to His death each day by our stand for truth.

Earthly blessings (i.e., material possessions, good times, friends, etc.) come and go. They were never meant to be permanent. The perspective of the Christian should be an eternal one. Jesus is enough for us to focus upward and not outward.

Jesus Is Enough Questions: What changes do you need to make to be content with the true blessings of Christ? How has your view shifted when you consider what Jesus considers "blessings?" What is the eternal impact of the eight virtues discussed (dependency on Jesus, brokenness over sin, contentment, right living, compassion, a heart for Jesus, unity, and hard times)?

_____

_____

_____

_____

_____

RECOMMITTING TO CHARACTER

I've learned it takes tremendous character to follow God fully and without compromise. God always puts His people in situations that test their character and integrity. These lessons serve to strengthen us for the days ahead so that our lives will give Him glory. But truly following Christ will cause every believer to have times of much joy but also of criticism and strain. Reforming to become more Christ-like will test the believer at a fundamental level. I had to answer the question once and for all: *Whom am I trying to please?* If man, the lesson below doesn't matter nearly as much. If Christ, the information below is critical.

Read Matthew 5:13–48

First, what is character?

Andy Stanley, in his book *Visioneering: fulfilling God's purpose through intentional living,* defines character this way: "The will to do what is right, as God defines right," regardless of personal cost.[1] This is a powerful statement. Our character is established when we first consider what God defines as right. Next, we actually have to do the "right" that God has declared. The last part is the most difficult. We have to do right even if the consequences will cost us. In other words, God's glory is more important that our comfort. To this definition of character, we should ask, "Who am I when no one is around?" If no one is around to see you, will you still do the right thing as God defines it? My point is simple: Our character is established by being like Christ.

Let's review what God says about integrity:

"Whoever walks in integrity walks securely, but he who makes his ways crooked will be found out." (Prov. 10:9)

"The integrity of the upright guides them, but the crookedness of the treacherous destroys them." (Prov. 11:3)

"The righteous who walks in his integrity—blessed
are his children after him!" (Prov. 20:7)

So based on the above Proverbs, a person who chooses character and integrity:

1. Lives securely, with no fear of public shame.
2. Lives with clarity, since principle guides 99 percent of his or her decisions.
3. Lives with less drama since a blessed life is a less stressed life.
4. Lives a life that will produce generational blessings.

Thoughts from the text:

1. Be the salt of the earth (v. 13)

   Salt does at least three things: it is a preservative, it adds flavor, and it produces thirst. By commanding us to be the salt of the earth, Christ is telling us to "preserve" or keep those around us from hurt through our words and living. He is also casting a compelling vision for the virtues of simple Christian living. The blessings that Christ describes are exciting! We should live in such a way that others want what we have!

2. Be the light of the world (vv. 14–15)

   In Scripture, light speaks to leadership. Since we are declared as His children, we are automatically leaders. Paul teaches us that we are the "light in the Lord" and we should walk accordingly. He goes on to say we should expose darkness for what it is. This is not the act of a follower, but a leader! What kind of light do you give off? Is it pure and bright or dim and flickering?

3. Be the example (v. 16)

   How you live will determine if you glorify God or shame him. Our first call is not to preach or teach. Our first call is not to build businesses or write books. Our first call is to live in a way that honors God so that others may see and emulate that life.

Christ goes on to illustrate in plain language what kingdom character looks like:

1. Character says we teach and lead others to do right (v. 19).
2. Character says we forgive quickly and restrain harsh words (vv. 21–22).
3. Character says we control our eyes and shield our hearts from inappropriate images (vv. 27–30).

4. Character says we honor our relationships with fidelity and lifelong commitment (vv. 31–32).
5. Character says we keep our commitments without having to be forced (vv. 33–37).
6. Character says we embrace servant leadership by consistently putting others before ourselves (vv. 38–42).
7. Character says we love and forgive our enemies, not just with words but also with action (vv. 43–48).

Jesus Is Enough **Questions:** How important is character to you? God is more concerned about your holiness than your happiness. When Christ becomes enough, His truth (expressed in love) is all that matters. Do you believe this? Is this the case in your life? If not, what is stopping you from transforming?

_____

_____

_____

_____

_____

_____

_____

_____

_____

_____

_____

_____

_____

_____

_____

LESSON
4

PREREQUISITES, PRAYER, AND PRIORITIES

By the mirror of the Word, we were slowly beginning to see ourselves more clearly. The Lord began to help us see "why" we pray, serve, and attend church. It wasn't easy to accept that much of what we do for God we do for selfish reasons. We pray, serve and attend church to get this or that from Him instead of simply wanting Him! Most of my Christian life, I had been subtly taught that God works for me. If I just pray hard enough, give enough, and be faithful, I can have whatever I want. During the process of learning that Jesus is enough, I discovered that *I work for God,* not the other way around!

Read Matthew chapter 6

The Condition of our hearts

Did you catch Jesus' description of the heart in verses 1 through 4? The heart with pure motives is what the Father desires. If your motive is Christ, you should experience consistency and steadfastness. If it is to show off, you will experience constant frustration. What is your motive for your service, your giving, and your church attendance? The Message Bible states Matthew 6:1–4 this way:

> Be especially careful when you are trying to be good so that you don't make a performance out of it. It might be good theater, but the God who made you won't be applauding. When you do something for someone else, don't call attention to yourself. You've seen them in action, I'm sure—"play actors" I call them—treating prayer meeting and street corner alike as a stage, acting compassionate as long as someone is watching, playing to the crowds. They get applause, true, but that's all they get.

Both public and private prayers are commanded in Scripture, but again, your motive is of intense interest to God. One of the ways our relationship with Christ gets deeper is our willingness to finally get real with God. Prayer is a time of communication between God and us. We should covet and protect our quiet time with Jesus by shutting everything out while communing with Him. Our prayers with Him should be intimate, heartfelt, and real.

How is your prayer life?

"Here's what I want you to do: Find a quiet, secluded place so you won't be tempted to role-play before God. Just be there as simply and honestly as you can manage. The focus will shift from you to God, and you will begin to sense his grace" (Matt. 6:6 MSG). Beware of tradition in prayer; words that roll out of you with no heart or thought behind them. Simply talk to Christ. Tell him how you feel and explain your struggles. Remember, God already knows what you need. He is aware of your pain and fears. Prayer is an opportunity to take those things to Him and find rest in that place.

The True Purpose of Prayer

Jesus gave us a beautiful model of how to build a relationship with Him through prayer. The Lord's prayer is often the first prayer we learn and the last prayer we model. To really pray the Lord's prayer requires a change of heart. One cannot read this prayer with understanding and walk away thinking about self. When you read this prayer, it will force you to:

1. Acknowledge God as your Father and submit to His "fatherly" authority (v. 9).
2. Acknowledge His holiness and your call to live holy as well (v. 9).
3. Submit to kingdom priorities and His will for your life (v. 10).
4. Be content with God's daily provision. The peace that flows from this is amazing (v. 11).
5. Experience brokenness from personal sin and commit to forgiving others (v. 12).
6. Trust God for victory in spiritual warfare. This requires that you engage in the battle (v. 13).
7. Submit yourself to the posture of worship (v. 13).

Priorities

From Matthew 6, Jesus gives us a few priorities that will help us with developing a heart for God and having pure motives. Verse 17 implies that fasting should be a normal part of the Christian's life. Not only is it a time to be intimate with Him but fasting helps you break fleshly holds and moves you into increased dependence upon Jesus. Just as every marriage needs occasional retreats, so we need these times alone with God.

We should also freely sow into the kingdom of God (vv. 19–24). Jesus is not condemning having a savings. He is correcting our view of money: Having all the money in the world but being unable to release it for kingdom purposes shows heart flaws. We live in darkness if we stay consumed with things we can see. Instead, Jesus is urging us to release what we have to things we cannot see. Again, Jesus is not discounting saving money. Instead, He is condemning consumerism (v. 22). The simple reality is that nothing will test your loyalty to God like money. It is a test we will face consistently for the rest of our lives.

Jesus declares in verses 25–32 that a simple life is the best life. He is not condemning setting goals, eating and dressing well. Jesus is teaching that when we become consumed with these things we lose focus and our hearts move away from God. When we live and think in more simple terms, we do not worry so often about things that mean nothing and miss out on the peace He offers. Worry never fixes anything (vv. 27, 31)!

Finally, "seek first the kingdom of God and his righteousness (v. 33)." A pure heart seeks God and His desires. Pure motives seek God's glory alone. So, instead of seeking things God already knows you need, develop an eternal perspective. Focus on kingdom things that really matter:

- your relationship with Christ, including holy and passionate living
- your love and care for your family
- your willingness to engage the forces of hell
- your love for and subsequent actions toward the lost
- your service and loyalty to the local church

Jesus Is Enough Questions: Think about "why" you do the things you do. How can you move your heart closer to Christ? What do you need to change to rightly see and serve Him?

_____
_____
_____
_____
_____

LESSON
5

LEADERSHIP LESSONS FROM THE ACTS 2 CHURCH

Every once in a while, we gather all the serving ministers and emerging leaders together for fellowship, teaching, and a meal. As our view of Christ was maturing, moving closer to the Acts 2 model became a priority. We knew that if Christ weren't enough for us as leaders, He would not be enough for the church as a whole.

Read Acts 2:40–47

When processing these verses years ago, I said this: "Friends, I have never felt this way about church and ministry before. The recent messages have been transforming for me. I'm even more convinced now that as leaders, we have to model the right mind-set and paradigm concerning Christ, His kingdom, and His church. It is critical that we as leaders understand what God has been saying to us—*that true and real Kingdom and blessings are on the inside.*"

The entire mind-set of *Jesus Is Enough* is built on the premise that the best blessings are inner ones. If the church is ever to recapture the true message of the kingdom, its leaders must understand that chasing worldly things only makes us more worldly; but pursuing heavenly things turns our hearts and minds toward Christ. From these verses, the leader can shift to the mind of Christ.

"Be saved from this perverse generation"

It is imperative that the leader set an example of purity and refuse to compromise on the Word of God or his lifestyle. Paul was bold enough to tell the Corinthians to "imitate me as I imitate Christ." He tells the Philippians to join in imitating him and to follow those who follow the example he has set. The Thessalonians were also advised that Paul purposefully gave himself to be an example of how to walk in the ways of Christ. Can you boldly tell others to follow you as you follow Christ? What are two or three areas that need to be cleaned up in your life? Why would change in this area be so hard?

"Continued steadfastly in doctrine"

The leader cannot be content with basic bible knowledge. Rather, he must keep pushing to learn and grow in the Word. In order for the "three thousand souls" to devote themselves and continue in the apostles teaching, the apostles had to hold fast to the doctrine they were taught. Can you articulate basic Christian doctrine to those you lead? How is your knowledge of Christian apologetics?

"Continued in fellowship, breaking of bread; breaking bread from house to house"

This activity was not just for the layperson! The leader must also take part in fellowship and even create opportunities for others to connect. The writer of Hebrews encourages his readers to stir up each other in love and good works and not neglect meeting together as some do (Heb. 10:24–25). The leader must also lead in this area if the Saints are to follow. How important is fellowship and hospitality to you? What are some things that need to stop so intentional fellowship can start?

"Continued in prayer"

I cannot emphasize enough the power of prayer. Prayer can defeat the Devil and save the sinner. It can strengthen the saint and heal the sick. Prayer can restore lost sheep and send laborers to the field. Prayer can even accomplish the impossible! For the leader, prayer can cultivate a relationship with Christ. Assess your prayer life honestly. If it is drudgery or feels forced, try to write down what it is in you that causes this. What needs to be done to get you in the habit of praying with others? Not just over food! Do you find yourself praying during the good and bad times?

"The fear came upon every soul"

There was an awe and reverence that the first century believers had for the Lord. Christ was everything to them, and reverence existed purely because He is God. The leader must truly reverence God, not just see Him as a means to an end. Jesus was truly enough. We have lost the fear of the God in today's church. To change this, leaders must fear God again more than they fear losing members or offending the culture. Ask three or four close friends if they think you really fear and reverence God in your daily living.

"Had all things in common; sold their possessions and goods"

The leader must be a good steward and understand the principle of giving. The best way to destroy selfishness and build up Christ-centered thinking is to become a giver. This thinking so permeated the early church that later in Acts 4, we see that the believers were of one heart and soul. These believers had so much in common; no one lacked anything. As leaders, we must cultivate the joy of blessing others. This week, find twenty-five dollars, fifty dollars, or one hundred dollars and give it to someone you think could use it.

"Gladness and singleness of heart"

True kingdom life stems from believers having a singleness of heart. There is one Lord, one Savior, and one church. There were no divisions, because Jesus was enough. Having a singleness of heart can lead to living a very simple and basic life in the Lord. The leader must embrace and demonstrate the real blessings that come from Jesus being enough. What are some things that you need to let go of to enjoy the simple life in Christ? Do you purposefully carve out time for simple things (i.e., going for a walk, sitting and thinking, playing with your kids, reading, etc.)?

"Praising God"

The leader understands how worthy God is of our praise. The leader also enjoys getting others to see how awesome and great Christ is. He feels it is his responsibility to lead others into giving Christ honor, praise, and worship. Write down three ways your life inspires others to love God. Do you have times during the week where you get into His presence and weep, clap, sing, or worship?

Jesus Is Enough **Questions:** What will you do to adjust your life to these principles?

_____
_____
_____
_____
_____
_____
_____
_____
_____
_____
_____
_____
_____
_____

$$\boxed{\begin{array}{c} \textbf{LESSON} \\ \textbf{6} \end{array}}$$

TO LIVE IS CHRIST!

Read Philippians chapter 1

Friends, what a joy it is to live in Christ Jesus! At this point, slowly but surely, we were freeing ourselves from our misunderstandings of kingdom and of what true blessings looked like. As the apostle Paul put it, "The kingdom of God is not eating and drinking, but righteousness and peace and joy in the Holy Spirit" (Rom. 14:17).

My goal was just Christ; just immersion in the Word for Christ's sake and for His glory alone. My preaching had become free of a need for "results." As blasphemous as this might sound, it was not tied to material blessings or meeting everyone's needs. I simply wanted Jesus! I came to believe that when we have Him and are focused on Him, all of our true and critical needs are met!

This revelation did not come without consequences. I was now meeting some resistance. Jesus simply isn't enough for many church people. I lost members over this message. However, the words of Paul in this chapter began to lift my spirit. I knew that even though there was a price to pay, I was on the right track!

Thoughts from the text:

1. Paul's pastoral prayer is an excellent model (vv. 3–5)

   How would our lives and attitudes change if we adopted Paul's pastoral prayer life and focus on fellowship? What would kingdom look like if we intentionally spent time remembering and praying for our brothers and sisters in Christ just out of sheer love? Paul's focus was Christ even in his suffering. What if we consistently encouraged each other that God's purpose for us still stands, even in suffering (vv. 6, 7)?

2. If kingdom is Christ, then kingdom is love (vv. 9–11)

   Our love for Jesus and people should be growing. However, it is not something we can just will to happen. That heart growth is a function of both knowledge (of the Word) and discernment (right application of the Word). Both will wither or be inconsistent if kingdom is outward rather than inward. Abounding love is fortified by right living (vv. 10–11). Why? Because our love for Christ must be developed first and proof of that love lies in our thoughts and behavior (John 14:15).

3. Kingdom is inward (vv. 12–14)

   Once again, kingdom manifestation is about who we are on the inside and the expression of God's eternal purpose. Paul clearly understood this. His jail cell was not a sign of sin, but success (v. 12)! His chains weren't "of" Christ; rather his chains were "in" Christ. Paul understood real blessings. As a result, everyone around him saw that he was imprisoned for Christ and believers were emboldened in the Spirit.

4. To live is Christ! (vv. 19–21)

   Now, *this* is the attitude of kingdom people! Real deliverance has a proper motive; to stand for Christ without shame and in boldness. Look at this attitude in Paul: in life or in death, may Christ get the glory! To live is Christ. If we die in Christ, that is gain! So again, who cares about a car, house, or boat?

5. Who you are will control what you do, especially in difficult times (vv. 27–30)

   "Only let your manner of life be worthy of the gospel of Christ …" If Christ is your life, your conduct will show it. If Christ is your life, you will connect with the local body and strive for "one spirit, one mind, and one faith in the gospel." If Christ is your life, then fear has been defeated! Seriously! Why fear death when death is conquered? If Christ is your life, the consumer in you must be corrected by the cross that we must bear. It is an inescapable and culturally uncomfortable reality that the apostles had this mind-set: "It is an honor to endure suffering for His sake."

Jesus Is Enough **Questions:** Christ should literally be your life. If this is true, how do express this on a daily basis? When times are both good and bad, does this heart show? If so, how do others see it in you? List some areas where you are still bound to earthy, circumstantial realities.

_____

_____

_____

_____

_____

_____

_____

_____

_____

_____

_____

LESSON 7

LEARNING TO LIVE LIKE CHRIST!

Read Philippians chapter 2

"To live is Christ, to die is gain!" We were learning that this declaration is fundamental for a truly kingdom-minded person. In essence, this was the opposite of what most kingdom talk was all about. This was the heart of people who were totally surrendered to Christ. As we will see, Christ modeled total surrender by humbling Himself even to the point of death on the cross. Learning to live like Christ (or living a kingdom life) includes embracing a sacrificial, totally obedient way of thinking and behaving. It includes understanding the strength required to walk in submission and humility. The kingdom-minded person's purpose is much greater than personal fulfillment. Let's dig in.

Thoughts from the text:

1. To live like Christ is to embrace covenant (vv. 1, 2)

    Paul is essentially saying that given all Christ has done, we should return His love by loving others. That is an expression of Kingdom and covenant. The Message Bible says it this way: "If you've gotten anything at all out of following Christ, if his love has made any difference in your life, if being in a community of the Spirit means anything to you, if you have a heart, if you care—*then do me a favor: Agree with each other, love each other, be deep-spirited friends*" (Phil. 2:1, 2).

    The truth is that Christ has consoled us, comforted us, and given us His Spirit. As members of the kingdom of God, we must *live* lives of unity. We must protect our covenants at all costs. We must not run *from* each other. Rather, we must run *to* each other.

2. To live like Christ is to die to selfishness (vv. 3, 4)

How can we hope to walk in the power of this passage when we can't even be unselfish in our prayers and living? How can this passage become a reality when we cannot see God's will as better than our own (i.e., give me this God, give me that Lord)? Again, The Message Bible states it clearly: "Don't push your way to the front; don't sweet-talk your way to the top. Put yourself aside, and help others get ahead. Don't be obsessed with getting your own advantage. Forget yourselves long enough to lend a helping hand. (Phil. 2:3, 4)"

This is why Christ must become enough. When He does, we can truly move into kingdom living.

3. To live like Christ is to reflect His character in our actions (vv. 5–11)

The word *let* in verse 4 implies that all we have to do is get out of the way. The Holy Spirit desires to develop this kind of heart in us. If we decide to think and act like Christ, selfish praying, declaring, naming and claiming, etc., will be swallowed up in our pursuit of the Father's will! He set aside worship for whippings, exaltation for execution, and glory for the grave. He humbled Himself for the sakes of others. This is how we should live. This is kingdom. Heavenly exaltation should be our goal, not earthly. While earthly success comes and goes, kingdom success is eternal by nature. Bowing the knee is symbolic of kingdom life. For this reason, we totally surrender to the plans and purposes of Christ. Amazingly, that posture produces the peace we all crave as well!

4. To live like Christ is to put Christ's character into action (vv. 12–30)

Consider the "action" in Paul's charge to the Philippians:

- Walk in obedience in the fear of God, even in the absence of authority (v. 12).
- Embrace God's sovereignty and His will, not your own (v. 13).
- Do everything readily and cheerfully; no bickering allowed (v. 14)!
- Understand that your character is on display for the world to see (v. 15)!
- Stay anchored in the Word (v. 16)!
- Rejoice, even when you are called to sacrificial living (vv. 17, 18)!
- Refuse to "seek your own," and succumb to the pressures of consumer culture (v. 21)!
- Live so people easily recognize your "proven worth" (v. 22).
- Walk as sons and daughters in the gospel and honor good leaders (vv. 22, 29).
- Realize that living like and for Christ may cost you your life (v. 30)!

Jesus Is Enough **Questions:** Have you begun to move beyond the consuming mind-set? Instead of Christ being a means to an end, are you seeing Him as the end? If not, what do you think you need to do to get there? How does your life reflect Christ's character?

_____

_____

_____

_____

_____

_____

_____

_____

_____

_____

_____

_____

_____

_____

_____

LESSON 8

LOSING ALL FOR CHRIST!

Well around this time, the rubber was introducing itself to the road. Some of those who saw where we were headed were a bit disgruntled. I still think they had hope that this was just a passing fad—a season I was going through, a mid-life crisis! How wrong they were! I had gotten to the point where I was willing to lose it all for Christ. Sure, I still had moments of fear and doubt like anyone else (and still do), but life was making more sense to me. Without embracing that Jesus is enough, how were Christians truly supposed to live with any lasting joy? How were we to face each day truly with all the pain of this fallen world on full display? How were we to stand for truth and righteousness when we knew God's message of holiness and redemption is normally rejected?

Read Philippians chapter 3:1-11

Sometimes, it is safe and needful to review what was previously taught so we get the message. Paul acknowledges this in the first verse, so let's do the same!

Remember, we have been feeling the Lord shifting us into a fresh kingdom understanding. We believe His desire is to move us away from searching the Word for a *blessing* to searching the Word for the *Blessor*. Christ is calling us to maturity, to be fully formed, to loving Him for His sake, not ours. *Even our thinking on what it means to be blessed has changed!* Consider the Beatitudes:

- Blessings flow in your dependency upon Jesus. Jesus taught that we should be poor in Spirit. Another way of putting this is being at the end of our spiritual rope. The result is very little you and much more of God.
- Blessings flow from brokenness—from those who mourn.
- Blessings flow from contentment and self-control. Jesus refers to this as "meekness" or "strength under control."

- Blessings flow from simple, right living. At the core, we should hunger and thirst for righteousness: Again, simple, right living.
- Blessings flow from true, godly compassion. To have compassion for God's creation is to reflect God's mercy.
- Blessings flow from the "pure in heart" or a heart that loves Jesus.
- Blessings flow from unity. Those who are truly blessed are those who find themselves as peacemakers.
- Blessings flow from how you handle hard times. The closer we get to Christ, the greater is the chance of being persecuted for righteousness sake.

Also from Matthew 5, Christ taught in plain language what kingdom character looks like:

- Character says we teach and lead others to do right.
- Character says we forgive quickly and restrain harsh words.
- Character says we control our eyes and shield our hearts from inappropriate images.
- Character says we honor our relationships with fidelity and lifelong commitment.
- Character says we keep our commitments without having to be forced.
- Character says we embrace servant leadership by consistently putting others before ourselves.
- Character says we love and forgive our enemies, not just with words but also with action.

So how can we perceive blessings the way Christ taught them? How can we develop the kind of character Christ spoke of? How can we embrace the declaration and truth of: "To live is Christ, to die is gain?" Answer: Embrace a joyful willingness to lose all for Christ!

1. Beware of people and thoughts that turn "success" in Christ into rules or worldly accomplishments (vv. 2–6).

In Paul's day there were many people whose teaching steered believers *away* from Christ and into man-made requirements. The same is true today. We must worship God in the Spirit and not fall for man's definition of success. Paul clearly understood this. He realized that success was in the Redeemer and not the total of his church plants. Do you truly, "put no confidence in the flesh?" In this context, that means your own abilities or accomplishments. The popular "believe in yourself" mantra is garbage, as Paul called it.

2. We must be willing to "Lose all for Christ" (vv. 7, 8)!

Simply to know God intimately is worth the loss of everything the *culture* tells us is important! Most of us don't even get close to this kind of holy zeal. Our lives are ruled by convenience and we get angry when we are asked to sacrifice. Not only should we "count all this as loss" we should view them as "rubbish." This speaks to the distance that should exist between Christ and His kingdom and other priorities. True kingdom "gain" is Christ!

3. Knowing Christ through faith-based righteousness is worth losing your life (vv. 9, 10)!

Compare Paul's kingdom mind-set to ours:

1. He wants to lose all for Christ; we want to gain all from Christ.
2. He views serving as success; we want to be served.
3. He rejoiced when he lost all things; we rejoice only when we gain things.
4. His goal was intimacy and obedience for Christ; our goal is to obey to get from Christ.

"[T]hat I may know him and the power of his resurrection, and may share his sufferings, becoming like him in his death, that by any means possible I may attain the resurrection from the dead." (Phil. 3:10–11, ESV)

We must be willing to count everything loss for Christ. Only then can we have everything with the right heart, motive, and perspective. That is kingdom.

Jesus Is Enough Questions: What needs to change to cause you to lose it all for Christ? Losing everything could include your money, physical freedom, status, or ministry.

_____
_____
_____
_____
_____
_____
_____
_____
_____
_____
_____

LESSON 9

PRESSING TOWARD CHRIST!

Read Philippians 3:12–21

Let's read the rest of the chapter in context to better understand kingdom. First let me say that most Christians love these passages of Scripture. So do I! It has brought me so much encouragement over the years. The thought of setting a goal and working toward it fires me up! What about you?

But consider these questions: What is Paul (in context) pressing toward? Why is he choosing to forget those things that are behind? What is the "mark" or "goal" he is pressing toward? What is the prize? What is the upward call of God in Christ Jesus? What is he willing to "lose all" for?

Thoughts from the text:

1. Paul's purpose for life and ministry is Christ! (v. 12)

   Paul wants what Christ wants. Christ "made him his own" for the purpose of Paul drawing closer to Him.

"But whatever gain I had, I counted as loss for the sake of Christ. Indeed, I count everything as loss because of the surpassing worth of knowing Christ Jesus my Lord. For his sake I have suffered the loss of all things and count them as rubbish, *in order that I may gain Christ* and be found in him, not having a righteousness of my own that comes from the law, but that which comes through faith in Christ, the righteousness from God that depends on faith—that I may know him and the power of his resurrection, and may share his sufferings, becoming like him in his death, that by any means possible I may attain the resurrection from the dead." (Phil. 3:7–11) [Emphasis mine]

When we say, "I press on," please remember what that "press" is about; to know Christ, to fulfill the will of Christ (not your own), to lose all for Christ, and to die for Christ if necessary!

2. Paul's past is forgotten in order to move toward Christ (v. 13)

We are all familiar with this verse. The imagery here is of a runner running a race. Looking backwards is the surest way to lose speed, get out of your lane, and lose the race. Yet, we do this all the time! We worry about our congregants, ministry and what others will say instead of pressing toward Christ. I wonder what would happen if we could forget the past for the sake of reaching ahead. Can you think of anything you would like to forget, and in its place put a future filled with Jesus?

3. Paul's press is toward Christ! (v. 14)

"I press on toward the goal for the prize of the upward call of God in Christ Jesus" (v. 14). The prize Paul references is an upward prize that God offers because of what Christ Jesus has done. Simply put, the "goal" is a Christlike life, devoted to His will and kingdom purpose. The "prize" is eternal life with Jesus forever. The "call" is an upward, heavenly call. So quoting this Scripture for personal, material gain is the exact opposite of its intended message. The context declares that our press should be an emptying of self for the sake of Christ and eternity.

4. Paul expects maturing Christians to have this mind-set (vv. 15, 16)

We discussed this in the previous lesson: Knowing Christ through faith-based righteousness is worth losing your life. All you should desire is Christ. All you should desire is the power that raised Him to life. All you should desire is to be raised to life like Christ did (cf. Phil. 3:10, 11).

5. Compare our cultural mind-set with Paul's Kingdom mind-set:

   • Paul wants to lose all for Christ. We want to gain all from Christ.
   • Paul views serving as success. We desire to be served.
   • Paul rejoiced when he lost all things. We tend to rejoice when we gain things.
   • Paul's goal was intimacy and obedience to Christ. Typically, we obey to get from Christ.

6. Walk with others who have this same mind-set (vv. 17–19)

Seek fellowship with those who have the mind of Christ. You should desire to be a person whose mind and heart are set on eternal things. Therefore, hang out with those who live the same way. We already know that consuming earthly things lead to destruction. 1 John teaches that the love of the Father cannot be in us if we chase after the world. If our god is our "belly" then what we "consume" will be more important than God. This is tough to hear for a materialistic culture.

7. Rejoice! Our citizenship is in heaven! (v. 20)

I dare you to compare what you are going through now, with heaven. I dare you! Imagine your lowly body being gloriously transformed like Christ's. Imagine the reward of no more pain, drama, or worldly mess! This was the purpose of Paul pressing toward the mark. For what are you pressing?

Jesus Is Enough Questions: What is your purpose in life? Can you honestly say that the beginning, middle and end of it is Christ? How has your understanding of "pressing toward the mark" changed? How will you live this out?

_____

_____

_____

_____

_____

_____

_____

_____

_____

_____

_____

_____

_____

_____

COVENANT, CONTENTMENT, CHARITY IN CHRIST!

Read Philippians chapter 4

As Paul brings this letter to a close, he outlines three kingdom principles we would do well to incorporate into our thinking and actions: covenant (unity), contentment (peace), and charity (giving). As it has been demonstrated over the last few lessons, the kingdom of God is less about what you own and more about who you are in Christ. These three principles are key markers of Christian maturity.

Principle 1: Covenant (Unity)

1. The atmosphere of covenant (v. 1)

    Consider the language Paul uses to describe the Philippians. He calls them "brothers." He loves and longs for them. They are not just common saints but a joy to Paul. This language demonstrates the love he had for them. To describe the Philippians as his "joy and crown" signifies the great value Paul placed upon their lives. There is no doubt that Paul considers himself a servant to his church. This is a covenant relationship based on love, service, and "standing firm" in the Lord.

2. The admonition of covenant (vv. 2, 3)

    Paul named names! In this passage, he directly asked two people to stop arguing and patch things up! He then requested that the process be facilitated by other saints with love and the right motive. It was as if Paul were saying, "Saints, you also have a responsibility to strengthen the hands of these two people." If only we were so bold today!

3. The attitude of covenant (vv. 4, 5)

"Rejoice in the Lord always; again I will say, rejoice. Let your reasonableness be known to everyone. The Lord is at hand." Translation: Be reverent, joyful, and gentle toward one another. This is urgent because the Lord is at hand. This reference was not indicating the Lord returning as in *time*. Rather, it was referencing "space"—the Lord is in our midst *now and is watching*. We should fight for unity with love and respect and do it now!

Principle 2: Contentment (Peace)

1. How Prayer produces Contentment (v. 6)

Before Paul tells his readers that he is content, he gives some directives on how that contentment is to be produced. The first is the ability to release our troubles and cares to Christ in prayer. Now this is a critical point: Contentment is released by the mere act of praying. We will become content when we release anxious thoughts to God! The text does not say God is obligated to answer the prayer the way we want. It simply says, don't be anxious—pray.

2. How Peace flows from Contentment (v. 7)

Again, it is the act of praying that released peace, not the desired results! The peace comes from knowing that God knows our hearts. Furthermore, peace comes when we are able to rest in His *sovereign will!* This verse says nothing about us getting a favorable answer to prayer. Amazingly, peace is spoken of as a "guard" of your two most sensitive areas: your heart and your mind. Have you noticed that without real peace, life becomes very difficult?

3. How what you Ponder affects Contentment (vv. 8, 9)

This isn't as deep as it sounds. We must control the things we listen to, watch, and read. We must be intentional about focusing on the true, noble, just, pure, lovely, of good report, virtuous, and praiseworthy from a biblical perspective. This kind of concentration brings and sustains contentment.

Principle 3: Charity (Giving)

1. Giving with the right motives (vv. 10–13)

Paul was content, but rejoiced when the church decided to support him and ensure he had all that he needed. The context demonstrates that Paul didn't demand from them or manipulate them. In fact, it seems he rejoiced because the giving was "free will" and flowed from their love and concern. Just because some have perverted this passage doesn't mean we aren't called to give with a loving heart. Nevertheless, the recipient of the gift must keep his/her focus on Christ and must never, ever "fleece the flock."

2. Giving with mission in mind (vv. 14–16)

Paul's life was all about advancing the gospel. As a result, the saints recognized that call and gave to support not just the man, but also the mission. The Philippians weren't giving to get a blessing. They were giving to invest in the kingdom of Christ. We are no different and must give in the same manner.

3. Giving is a mark of maturity (vv. 17–20)

Paul describes giving with Old Testament worship language. He described their giving as "a sweet-smelling aroma, an acceptable sacrifice that pleases God." Temple sacrifices were described this way (Exodus 29:18, Leviticus 3:5 and many more). Christ's bodily sacrifice was described as "a fragrant offering and sacrifice to God" (Eph. 5:2). Even the description of the prayers of the saints in the great tribulation used this language (Rev. 8). Paul desired that the saints gave for spiritual reasons. In context, the primary fruit he refers to is intimacy with God. The secondary fruit is the provision of earthly "needs." When we give with the right motive (to worship, not give to get) and with mission in mind (caring for our leaders, the church, and advancing the mission of the kingdom), we move toward our kingdom destiny.

Jesus Is Enough Questions: How are these principles playing out in your life? How is the reality that Jesus is your all and all affecting your relationship with others, your ability to be content, and your willingness to pour your resources into the kingdom?

_____
_____
_____
_____
_____
_____
_____
_____
_____
_____

LESSON
11

WHAT IS FAITH?

In lesson 10, I mentioned that peace and joy flow out of submitting our hearts and requests to God, and trusting in Him for His desired outcome not ours. This is foundational to truly understanding that *Jesus is enough!* However, I understand that this mind-set crashes against modern concepts of faith, particularly if you travel in "Spirit-filled" circles as I do. So, let's take a few weeks to consider this issue of faith.

One of the critical aspects of our paradigm shift toward Christ (and away from the unbalanced pursuit of His stuff) centers on the question, "What is faith?" I believe it is important to "re-study" this very topic and sort through certain Scriptures to make sure we understand them correctly. Here are a few that represent the sort of passages we sometimes misinterpret.

- Matthew 17:20: So Jesus said to them, "Because of your unbelief; for assuredly, I say to you, if you have faith as a mustard seed, you will say to this mountain, 'Move from here to there,' and it will move; and nothing will be impossible for you."
- John 14:13–14: And whatever you ask in My name, that I will do, that the Father may be glorified in the Son. If you ask anything in My name, I will do it.
- John 15:7: If you abide in Me, and My words abide in you, you will ask what you desire, and it shall be done for you.

As a reminder, a Bible teacher's primary responsibility is to learn how to properly interpret and communicate Scripture. This is accomplished by understanding and using key elements of interpretation. These elements include understanding over-arching biblical principles, scriptural harmony, context, and understanding types and grammar. Overarching principles include God's power (His sovereignty), God's person (His character), and God's plan. We must never interpret Scripture in a way that is contrary to how these facets of God are laid out in the Word. God's power, person, and plan keep us straight. The principle of scriptural harmony causes us to interpret Scripture in light of other Scripture. Biblical context prompts us to read Scripture in light of the passage, chapter, and book. Context also includes understanding the setting and background of the text. The types principle recognizes that there are copies or patterns in Scripture of something greater. Finally, we must read Scripture as it was meant to be read grammatically. Understanding these principles will put us on the right track for understanding scripture. Even if we don't know quite what a passage means, we can know what it doesn't mean through a process of elimination. Let's apply some of these principles to the passages we previously listed.

We can easily say that the above Scriptures aren't blank checks for us to dream up what we want and make God obligated to do it. Why? Because He is sovereign and we are not. His character is perfect and ours is not (which is why we sometimes "ask amiss" according to James 4:3). His plan is primary; ours is not. We would violate the overarching facet of God's sovereignty if we believe God must bend to our every desire. Scriptural harmony also helps us out:

- 1 John 5:14: Now this is the confidence that we have in Him, that if we ask anything *according to His will*, He hears us.

Implied in the above passage and in others like it are the sovereignty, character, and plan of God. As John Macarthur rightly put it, "To ask in Jesus' name does not mean to tack such an expression on the end of a prayer as a mere formula. It means: (1) the believer's prayer should be for God's purposes and kingdom and not selfish reasons; (2) the believer's prayer should be on the basis of God's merits and not any personal merit or worthiness; and (3) the believer's prayer should be in pursuit of His glory alone."

Jesus Is Enough **Questions:** Is praying in this manner faith filled or faithless and why? How should these thoughts change both your prayers and the effect circumstances have on your joy?

_____
_____
_____
_____
_____
_____
_____
_____
_____
_____
_____

LESSON
12

WHAT IS FAITH? PART 2

This whole issue of seeking His will is mighty challenging, isn't it? There is so much that God allows that we do not understand. I suppose that's why the thought of "taking charge" of our lives and "making it happen" is so appealing to us. To think that we are not in control and the course of our lives is not determined by us alone is a frightening thought. I've been known to say on occasion that our decisions determine our destiny. In other words, when we decide to obey God, we end up in the place God wants us to be. This also means that we will have the level of outward success that He wants us to have. Simply following Christ with faithfulness and integrity makes us successful! So, God's measure of success begins first with who we are.

It is my contention that faith is not aggressively trying to take charge and move God. It is my belief that true faith flows from a surrendering to God's sovereign purpose; a relinquishing of our personal plans, goals, and dreams, and a bold declaration of "not my will, Father, but Thy will be done." Indeed, this is the ultimate expression of faith. But this thought is so despised by some that bizarre teachings have arisen to counter it. For example, the teaching that faith is a force—supposedly expressed in Hebrews 11:1:

"Now faith is the assurance of things hoped for, the conviction of things not seen."

It is believed by some that the word *substance* implies that faith is a literal thing; a force or energy that originates in the heart, comes out of the mouth, and creates the reality of the words that are spoken. Supposedly, words of faith activate God and words of fear activate Satan, which is why one is taught to never "speak death" into one's life by using negative confessions. Rather, as the teaching goes, we should speak what we want into existence. Sounds mighty new age to me!

The truth is that faith "is being sure of what we hope for and certain of what we do not see" (NIV). The word *substance* is from the Greek *hypostasis*, which simply means "an assurance; a confidence." Faith is simply knowing that God has a plan for you, agreeing that His plan is best, and trusting in Him fully for the execution of His plan, not ours. I love the way Solomon put it:

"Trust in the LORD with all your heart, and do not lean on your own understanding. In all your ways acknowledge him, and he will make straight your paths." (Prov. 3:5, 6)

So it is not what we want but what He wants. That is faith. Living a life of complete surrender requires extreme levels of faith. Interestingly, when we read the rest of Hebrews 11 and examine what the heroes of faith trusted God for, we find without exception that God's will (not their own) was their priority. We also find that although some prospered in their circumstances, some "died in faith, not having received the promises, but having seen them afar off were assured of them" (Heb. 11:13). Others "were tortured, not accepting deliverance, that they might obtain a better resurrection. Still others had trial of mockings and scourgings, yes, and of chains and imprisonment. They were stoned, they were sawn in two, were tempted, were slain with the sword. They wandered about in sheepskins and goatskins, being destitute, afflicted, tormented—of whom the world was not worthy. They wandered in deserts and mountains, in dens and caves of the earth. And all these, having obtained a good testimony through faith, did not receive the promise, God having provided something better for us, that they should not be made perfect apart from us" (Heb. 11:35–40).

I praise you, Father, because You provided something better for us: the promise all these heroes of faith trusted in and waited for, *Jesus Christ.*

Jesus Is Enough **Questions:** How do you feel about this? How does it make you feel to know that many times in Scripture, "receiving" was not the issue, but faithfulness was the issue?

_____

_____

_____

_____

_____

_____

_____

_____

_____

_____

_____

_____

_____

WHAT IS FAITH? PART 3

After one Sunday service, while teaching through the book of Philippians, I turned on the TV and flipped to the all-Christian station. I had just spent the morning attempting to reorient our interpretation of Paul's classic statement, "I press toward the goal for the prize of the upward calling in Christ Jesus." I wanted our congregants to see that the prize was in Christ Jesus and not our personal goals! I was saddened by what I saw on the TV. There was a very prominent and influential teacher who was teaching hundreds of thousands of people that our words have creative power, that faith is a force, and that God will create our words if we give more, believe stronger, and say the words over and over again. Wow.

Earlier, I promised more thoughts on James chapter 4. In particular, this passage is particularly instructive:

"You ask and do not receive, because you ask wrongly, to spend it on your passions."

One of the primary reasons I'm committed to viewing faith through *surrendered* rather than *self-centered* lenses is what is taught in this passage and in its context. Let's read it in that context:

> What causes quarrels and what causes fights among you? Is it not this, that your passions are at war within you? You desire and do not have, so you murder. You covet and cannot obtain, so you fight and quarrel. You do not have, because you do not ask. You ask and do not receive, because you ask wrongly, to spend it on your passions. You adulterous people! Do you not know that friendship with the world is enmity with God? Therefore, whoever wishes to be a friend of the world makes himself an enemy of God. Or do you suppose it is to no purpose that the Scripture says, "He yearns jealously over the spirit that he has made to dwell in us?" But he gives more grace. Therefore it says, "God opposes

the proud, but gives grace to the humble." Submit yourselves therefore to God. Resist the devil, and he will flee from you. (James 4:1–7 ESV)

James is trying to teach his readers that the reason they sometimes don't receive has to do with the state of their hearts. James is trying to correct greed, selfishness, and self-centeredness and move his readers toward God's agenda, not their own.

Implicit in the passage is a condemnation of his readers' motive for asking. Their asking was about personal blessings and material, worldly gain. The key to correcting this heart defect according to James is simply to "submit" or surrender to God. This would then correct this faulty prayer practice and inaccurate view of faith. Even more powerful is that submission thwarts satanic plans and produces intimacy with God (James 4:8)!

Go James! You preach on preacha', preacha'!

Jesus Is Enough **Questions:** Have you ever "asked wrongly?" How often do you think you pray with your desires as the primary motivator rather than the will of God? How will submission to the will of God change your prayer life?

_____

_____

_____

_____

_____

_____

_____

_____

_____

_____

_____

_____

_____

_____

_____

_____

```
┌─────────────────┐
│     LESSON      │
│       14        │
└─────────────────┘
```

CHRISTOLOGY

Let's begin our study in the book of Colossians. Written to this church in Phrygia by the apostle Paul from prison, this letter is rich in the lordship and centrality of Christ over all creation, and the implications thereof.

Read Colossians 1:1-18

Now more than ever, Christians need to educate themselves on the basics. We have slid so far into cultural Christianity that we barely know who Jesus is anymore. The focus must be on reorienting Christians back toward the Master instead of what is on the Master's table. However, this is a challenge. In our culture, doctrine is considered boring. Truth is relative. Essentials of the faith are unnecessary. As long as one can get one's blessing, the preaching is anointed. But if the focus is on Christ … if the focus is on defending the faith, walking in a way that honors Christ, studying Christ in His fullness and preparing to present the preeminent Christ to the hurting, the church must be dead.

Interestingly, the apostles didn't think this way as you've seen over the last few lessons. Rather than writing about how we can achieve our personal miracles, the apostles wrote extensively about our inheritance in Christ, living in holiness, rejecting worldly influence, being faithful, and refuting false doctrine. Take the book of Colossians for example. Written by Paul (again, from a Roman prison cell), the letter to the church of Colossae was written to reestablish basic Christian doctrine. The letter was written in response to the false teachers and their teachings that were negatively impacting the church. Colossae was struggling against:

1. An early form of Gnosticism, which taught that Jesus was less than God and not fully human, that the things needed to make one happy were secret and could only be gained through Gnostic thinking, and that all matter was evil.

2. Another variant of Gnosticism, which said that because of grace you could live how you want! What you do with your body has no effect on your spiritual life! Sound familiar?
3. Legalism: circumcision was necessary for salvation, Old Testament rituals must be practiced, etc.
4. Mysticism: the worship of angels, etc.

We are in a similar predicament. People are starving for truth, but they don't know what to believe anymore. In the absence of leadership, people will make up "truth" to soothe their tired souls. Clearly, we are in a battle for truth. That is why our study needs to shift from the consumer mind-set to Christ. Far from the pursuit of personal blessings, let's continue to pursue the Blessor. Christianity is more than God meeting your earthly needs (although I'm so glad He does that). Christianity is about glorifying God through the fruit we bear in Christ. Let's fight!

Thoughts from the text:

1. Be an Epaphras (vv. 1–8)

    Paul did not plant the church at Colossea, but a disciple of his (Epaphras) likely did. However, the growth of the church was evident. They heard the Word, learned the Word and bore fruit! What have you done with the Word you have learned? If it has been used solely for selfish gain, that will be evident. Is there Kingdom fruit *outside* of your personal life? The need for people with "the spirit of Epaphras" is critical. Not only did he plant and lead this church, but he was so concerned about the invasion of the truth snatchers (false teachers), he traveled all the way to Rome for Paul's help. For most of us, all we need to do is read a book or two!

2. Mature in Christ (vv. 9–14)

    Spiritual formation (or maturity in Christ) should be the highest aim for ourselves and for those we pray for and lead. Before giving them the motive, Paul gave them the method. It applies to us too if we want to win this battle:

    a. We should want Christ's will, not our own. True wisdom and understanding are always connected to His will.
    b. We should want to fully please the Lord through how we live.
    c. We should bear fruit if we are in Christ (v. 10; cf. John 15 and Galatians 5).
    d. We should study the Word to increase our knowledge of God.
    e. We should live lives of joyful patience through the power of God. This implies we won't always get what we want when we want.

f. We should give thanks anyway, not because we have all our earthly wants but because we have an inheritance with the Saints! We have been delivered from darkness, our sins have been forgiven, and we are set into the kingdom of Christ!

3. Know Christ well—Christology (vv. 15–19)

To bolster biblical truth, we must know well the God we serve. Paul points out a few things in these verses. Far from being less than God, Jesus Christ is the fullness of God! "He is the image of the invisible God—meaning "exactly like God." Adam was made in God's image, but only Christ could perfectly reflect visibly the invisible God! Also note that "firstborn," in this context, does not mean He is a created being; it means He is preeminent or highest in rank. David was called the firstborn (Ps. 89:27), but he was neither the first of Jesse's sons nor the first king of Israel. He was however, Israel's greatest king. Jesus cannot be created if He created all things. Paul continues by declaring that Jesus if fully God and the creator of all things (v. 16). Jesus is eternal and sustains the universe by His power (v. 17). Lastly, Jesus is head of the church, fully human, and the first to rise from the dead never to die again (v18).

4. Christ's priorities must be our priorities (v. 18)

Since Christ is the Head of the church, our priorities must be His priorities. Consider the following:

- "'Teacher, which is the great commandment in the Law?' And he said to him, 'You shall love the Lord your God with all your heart and with all your soul and with all your mind. This is the great and first commandment. And a second is like it: You shall love your neighbor as yourself.'" (Matt. 22:36–39)
- "And Jesus came and said to them, 'All authority in heaven and on earth has been given to me. Go therefore and make disciples of all nations, baptizing them in the name of the Father and of the Son and of the Holy Spirit, teaching them to observe all that I have commanded you. And behold, I am with you always, to the end of the age.'" (Matt. 28:18–20)

The above realities should cause change in us. It should call us to worship purely because God died so we could live. Reorienting ourselves toward Christ should both compel and convict us to repent and start over. What have you done with this knowledge? Have you shrunk the manifestation and mission of Christ to your needs alone? The power of the Holy Spirit will cause change in our lives and the lives of others.

Jesus Is Enough **Questions:** Describe how you feel when reading Colossians 1:15–18. Do you find that your perspective on life shifts while reading them? How do the truths contained in these verses compare to a car, or a house, or having lots of money? Can you see where joy actually comes from?

_____

_____

_____

_____

_____

_____

_____

_____

_____

_____

_____

_____

_____

_____

_____

CHRISTOLOGY, PART 2

Read Colossians 1:19–20

In lesson 14, we learned that the book of Colossians was written to refute false teaching and encourage the believers in Colossae to stay rooted in proper doctrine. As a result, the apostle Paul begins his letter exhorting the saints to both live for and get to know this Jesus that they have committed their lives to. I believe his goal was to produce an environment in which their spiritual foundation was so solid, that a few things would occur naturally:

1. They would have the right foundation from which to present Christ to others.
2. Their daily walk of holiness, faith, and wisdom would please God.
3. They would recognize false doctrine and as a result refuse to accept it and limit damage to the church.

It is critical for Christians to be armed with the truth and be able to communicate that truth with love and with respect. We are called to "contend for the faith that was once for all delivered to the saints. For certain people have crept in unnoticed who long ago were designated for this condemnation, ungodly people, who pervert the grace of our God into sensuality and deny our only Master and Lord, Jesus Christ" (Jude 3, 4).

So our reorientation away from consumerism to Christ is a necessary step to embrace a biblical worldview, see the importance of doctrine, and to fulfill the Great Commission. If we truly are expecting God to produce a harvest through our leadership and labor, we had better know the true nature of this God we are preaching! Let's quickly discuss the divine nature of Jesus and the Holy Trinity.

Jesus is God and man!

Always remember that Christ is fully God *and* fully man. Jesus is God in human flesh. He is not a mix of half God and half man but fully divine and fully human. These two natures (divine and human) are distinct and are never combined. They are separate yet act as a unit in the one person of Jesus. This is called the Hypostatic Union. I like what Matt Slick, founder of Christian Apologetics and Research Ministry (CARM) says on his website:

> One of the most common errors that non-Christian cults make is not understanding the two natures of Christ. For example, the Jehovah's Witnesses focus on Jesus' humanity and ignore His divinity. They repeatedly quote verses dealing with Jesus as a man and try and set them against scripture showing that Jesus is also divine. On the other hand, the Christian Scientists do the reverse. They focus on the scriptures showing Jesus' divinity to the extent of denying His true humanity. For a proper understanding of Jesus and, therefore, all other doctrines that relate to Him, His two natures must be properly understood and defined. [1]

God in Three Persons

Here is the doctrine of the Holy Trinity as succinctly as possible: In the entire universe, there is but one God who created that universe *ex nihilo,* which means "out of nothing." Within the nature of the one true and living God, there are three coequal and eternal persons (cognizant egos) existing simultaneously. The whole, undivided essence of God belongs equally to each of the three persons; God the Father; God the Son—who is Christ Jesus of Nazareth—and God the Holy Spirit. These three persons are one God. For a good study on the nature of Jesus and the Holy Trinity, visit www.carm.org and review the section on doctrine.

Although much of the church world thinks this kind of teaching is boring and doesn't meet any immediate needs, I believe it is critical to your joy and faith. This kind of teaching is foundational if we are to communicate Christ's love and reconciliation with a generation that rejects truth. *Having peace with God can only come through Jesus and His cross* (v. 20). The ability to stand on this truth is sorely lacking today. Read Acts 2:14–41 as a supplement to this lesson. Note how Peter was not concerned with getting anything from God. Instead, he laid a foundation of whom Christ was in relation to sin. It was the Gospels.

> Now I would remind you, brothers, of the gospel I preached to you, which you received, in which you stand, and by which you are being saved, if you hold fast

to the word I preached to you—unless you believed in vain. For I delivered to you as of first importance what I also received: *that Christ died for our sins in accordance with the Scriptures, that he was buried, that he was raised on the third day in accordance with the Scriptures.* (1 Cor. 15:1–4) [Emphasis mine]

Friends, "without controversy, great is the mystery of godliness: God was manifested in the flesh, Justified in the Spirit, seen by angels, preached among the Gentiles, believed on in the world, received up in glory" (1 Tim. 3:16).

Jesus Is Enough Questions: How should this reality affect you each day? How does it help you refute errors that may have crept into your thinking about life, doctrine, and faith?

_____

_____

_____

_____

_____

_____

_____

_____

_____

_____

_____

_____

_____

_____

LESSON
16

CONTENDING FOR CHRIST

Read Colossians 1:21–2:23

Dear readers, I'm convinced that if we really understood what Christ did and who we are in Him, we would live differently. Too many of us live "in chains" when we don't have too. That sense of bondage to sin and circumstances promotes a perceived inability to live in the freedom Christ purchased for us and offers to us daily. This perceived lack of freedom causes:

- feelings of condemnation, which limits action
- thoughts filled with hopelessness, which limits faith
- bondage to circumstances, which limits joy

Now more than ever, Christians need to educate themselves on the basics. We have slid so far into cultural Christianity we barely know who Jesus is anymore. We must reorient Christians back toward the Master instead of what is on the Master's table. However, this is a challenge. In our culture, doctrine is considered boring. Truth is relative. Essentials of the faith are considered unnecessary. As long as one can get a blessing, the preaching is anointed. But if the focus is on Christ, defending the faith, walking in a way that honors Christ, studying Christ in His fullness or preparing to present the preeminent Christ to the hurting, the church must be dead. So the theory goes.

Christianity is being assaulted from all sides: vain philosophies, paganism, atheism/agnosticism, and even relativism and pantheism. People are starving for truth, but they don't know what to believe anymore. In the absence of leadership, people will make up "truth" to soothe their tired souls. *We are in a battle for truth.* That's why our study needs to shift from the consumer mind-set to Christ. Far from the pursuit of personal blessings, let's continue to pursue the Blessor. Christianity is more than God meeting your earthly needs, although I'm so glad He does that! *Christianity is about glorifying God through the fruit we bear in Christ.* We who have been reconciled from evil deeds

(Col. 1:21–23) must engage in this battle! *Let's fight (struggle, strive, or contend) for Christ!*

Thoughts from the text:

1. To contend for Christ, we must press into areas of suffering and sacrifice. (Col. 1:24–25)

    Christ's enemies weren't satisfied with His death. They were intent on hurting his followers too. Jesus told us we'd have a cross to bear. We often times associate that cross with personal circumstances. It might be that many of those crosses are ours instead of His. How many of us are actually bearing a cross for His gospel? Every Christian is a commissioned steward of the gospel and therefore a cross bearer. How is your stewardship of the gospel?

2. To contend for Christ, we must love and be willing to "strive" for those we don't even know. (Col. 1:26–2:3)

    We must strive through study of the "mystery." This requires intense discipline and focus. Our hearts should be striving to preach and warn "every man." Only when our love for the lost overrides our fear of confrontation will we begin to contend for Christ in our evangelism. All of this requires a selfless attitude toward others. When we strive to put down selfish pursuits, we become like Paul in our text. Paul's life and labor was for the benefit of others. Paul longed to see the maturity in others. When we contend for Christ, these things will be a lifelong goal for us! (2:1–3)

3. To contend for Christ, we must familiarize ourselves with the false teachings of the day and get equipped to lovingly answer and refute them. (2:4–9)

    As a reminder, this epistle was written by Paul (again, from a Roman prison cell) to reestablish and reaffirm basic Christian doctrine and in response to false teachers threatening the church (See lesson 14 for the specific issues Colosse was facing). Think through these terms: "Walk in Him," "rooted and built up," and "established and abounding in the faith." What do they suggest to you? Persuasive words and thoughts are everywhere. For the believer, it is not enough to know truth from false. We must be equipped to convince and persuade men! First Peter 3:15 tell us that we should *always* be ready to explain the hope that is in us!

4. To contend for Christ, we must live in Christ. (2:11–15)

    We must embrace the fact that our bondage to our sinful nature has been "cut" away! Your living must reflect the completed sacrifice of Christ that "raised you up," "made you alive," "forgave all your trespasses," and "wiped out" your debt to the law! Since Christ has "disarmed" all authority and triumphed, so have you! This frees you to truly live in Him, full of love and not fear, full of holiness and not sin, full of joy and not despair! Embrace your new life and live it fully. Fight for the Christ that fought for you!

5. To contend for Christ, we must rightly embrace our freedom in Christ. (2:16–23)

We must never return to ceremonial legalism because none of us can keep the Law perfectly. This however does not mean we use our freedom to engage in disobedience. (Rom. 6:15, Gal. 5:13) It means that our freedom causes us to love the one who gave us grace. We are called to "hold fast to the Head" and by extension, His Word. We must not allow man-made traditions to "make the Commandment of God of no effect." (Matt. 15:6) Your freedom in Christ is the basis for the fight for truth.

Jesus Is Enough **Questions:** Are you contending for Christ? Have you taken the time to learn basic apologetics so you can defend the truths of Scripture? How should the *Jesus Is Enough* mind-set help you do this?

_____

_____

_____

_____

_____

_____

_____

_____

_____

_____

_____

_____

_____

_____

_____

LESSON
17

REFRESHING YOUR FOCUS

Read Colossians 3:1–11

Friends, this lesson begins with the issue of focus: what your heart seeks and where your mind is set. It has been my contention for months that *Jesus is enough*. He should be our focus and our ultimate blessing and breakthrough. Instead of focusing on worldly issues and material things, our short time on this earth is better spent focusing on Him alone. I know God backs me up in this because I see his confirmation. Everything we've read as we've moved through the Scriptures has pointed us back to Christ and His all-sufficient sacrifice. Jesus said, "Do not lay up for yourselves treasures on earth, where moth and rust destroy and where thieves break in and steal; but lay up for yourselves treasures in heaven, where neither moth nor rust destroys and where thieves do not break in and steal. *For where your treasure is, there your heart will be also.*" (Matt. 6:19–21) [Emphasis mine]

If our focus remains on earthly things, how can we reap a heavenly harvest? How can we bring in a divine harvest if we are not focused on the Lord of the harvest? Remember, the harvests that interest Christ are: (1) our lives and how we live them to His glory, and (2) our willingness to preach and make disciples. Everything else is secondary. Once our focus is correct, the kind of joy, peace, contentment, relationship healing, and Kingdom effectiveness that will flow in our lives will simply be amazing!

Thoughts from the text:

1. We must seek heavenly things (v. 1)

   How much clearer does the Holy Spirit have to be? We have been tricked into thinking that the kingdom of God is about what we can gather on earth. Wrong! *"For the kingdom of God is not a matter of eating and drinking but of righteousness and peace and joy in the Holy Spirit."* (Rom. 14:17) Your heart should desire "those things which are above where Christ is." But we rarely desire the "best" but prefer the temporal and perishable. I agree with the songwriter who wrote, "I just want to be where you are, living daily in your presence,"

2. We must develop an eternal focus (v. 2)

We preachers have not helped our congregants much with developing an eternal focus. In most cases, sermons are about earthly—instead of heavenly—things. Please understand that if your treasure is Christ, your heart (and therefore your actions) will reflect that. Remember, your heart directs your words and actions (cf. Matt. 15:18–20).

3. Your Christ focus is based on your death and resurrection in Christ (v. 3)

Everything (and I mean everything) earthly that you are dealing with *is nothing* compared to the blessing of eternal life! Please understand, internalize, and live this. The joy and hope in the Christian life is summarized in verse 4: *Christ is our life and we'll be with Him in glory*!

4. Being Christ focused brings increased holiness (vv. 5, 8–9)

The more we are Christ focused, the more things around us begin to change. Our text tells us that we are free from a host of impure things:

1. Fornication: Immortality; any form of sexual sin
2. Uncleanness: Impurity; immorality, evil thoughts and intentions
3. Passion/Evil desire: Sexual lust
4. Covetousness: Greed; the insatiable desire to gain more
5. Anger: A deep smoldering bitterness
6. Wrath: An outburst of sinful anger
7. Malice: Moral evil or wickedness
8. Blasphemy: In this context, slander against others
9. Filthy Language: You know what this means!
10. Lying: This too!

5. Since we've escaped God's wrath, let's live like it! (vv. 6, 7)

We used to covet and walk in idolatry (putting things above God). But not anymore right? This is critical: even your pursuit of *good* earthy things must not come before your pursuit of and focus on Christ.

6. Understand the core of being a "new man" (or woman) (v. 10)

The mind of a new creature doesn't stay in the mind but translates into action. It effects how we think and live. There should be a Holy Spirit empowered difference in our thoughts, words, pursuits, and actions than those of the unregenerate. An unregenerate mind focuses on self and world. A renewed mind centers on Christ and His cross. Sadly, many within the church seek the same kind of things the world does.

7. Christ is all and in all! (v. 11)

Simply put, Christ is your life! He alone is your central focus. Not a personal desire, a car, house, job, or even pain we've suffered should be central. Only Christ. It should be noted that the phrase "Christ is all, and is in all" does not teach universalism. In context, it teaches the fallacy of racism and sexism. One's race or social status does not lessen the mercy and grace of God in salvation.

Jesus Is Enough Questions: Where you place your attention greatly effects how you live your life. What does "Christ-focus" mean to you? How do you live this out? Why is it so difficult for most of us to keep our minds and hearts fixed on heavenly things?

_____

_____

_____

_____

_____

_____

_____

_____

_____

_____

_____

_____

_____

_____

LESSON
18

RECONNECTING WITH FAMILY

Read Colossians 3:12–25

Nothing can inhibit your ability to walk in the truths of Christ like family or relationship drama. Colossians is particularly good at helping us with this because of its laser-like focus on Christ. I believe with all my heart that for most Christian couples, singles, and parents, little therapeutic help is needed. What most of us need is more Christ in these areas. I thought seriously about conducting a marriage, singles, or parenting style seminar with this message. My focus would be on needs, communication, validation, relational principles, etc. Ultimately, I believe it is God's will to instead teach these verses in light of the *overall* context of why Paul was writing to the church of Colossae.

Spend a few moments re-reading:

- Colossians 1:15–20
- Colossians 1:27–28
- Colossians 2:6–7
- Colossians 3:1–2, 11

If anything, Colossians speaks to the preeminence of Christ and challenges us to look at everything through "Jesus" lenses as opposed to "please us" lenses. So, as we look at our text, we must consider the context.

Reconnection Points:

1. Because Christ *"is all and in all"* (3:11), you can walk in kingdom relational principles (vv. 12, 13). If your mind is set on Him, you have the anointed ability to forgive, be kind, be humble, and be patient in every relational circumstance.

2. Because *"you were raised with Christ"* (3:1), you are free to love (v. 14). This sounds simple but is very profound. You no longer have to place conditions on your love.

3. If *His peace rules* (v. 15), depression and fear cannot! Your Christ has "disarmed principalities and powers" (2:15). Did you know that your peace in marriage, singleness, and parenting is Christ-based rather than circumstantial?

4. His Word should be like contact lenses, inspiring us to conduct ourselves properly. (v. 16) A "rich, indwelt" Word brings wisdom, knowledge, worship, and grace. Every wife, husband, single person, and parent *needs* all of the above. Why? Because all of the above ensures a Savior rather than a self-focus.

5. Given the context up to this point, we give our all based on Christ and His work (v. 17). Motive is a powerful thing. If your motive is to walk in relationship for Christ's glory, you now have the key to forgiveness, joy, perseverance, etc. But if your motive turns selfish, "pride comes before the fall." (Prov. 16:18)

So what preceded verses 18–21 is as critical as the verses themselves. As a matter of fact, how can we understand these relationship verses without their intended "Christ first" context?

Some Quick Relationship Thoughts:

- "Wives, submit to your husbands, as is fitting in the Lord" (v. 18). View submission through the cross of Christ. The only thing that will prevent a woman from submitting to a godly man is seeing submission first through self and second through the Savior. Christ submitted to death by putting his Father first.
- "Husbands, love your wives, and do not be harsh with them" (v. 19). View love through the cross of Christ. The only thing that will prevent a man from loving a godly woman is seeing love first through self and second through the Savior. Christ loved unto death by putting his Father first.
- "Children, obey your parents in everything, for this pleases the Lord. Fathers, do not provoke your children, lest they become discouraged" (vv. 20, 21). View parental relationships through the cross of Christ. Discipline *and* love. Rebuke *and* encourage. Exercise patience, forgiveness, hope. Honor your *parents*, and love your *children*. Reaffirm that children are a blessing and a heritage from the Lord (Ps. 127:3).
- "Bondservants, obey in everything those who are your earthly masters, not by way of eye-service, as people-pleasers, but with sincerity of heart, fearing the Lord" (v. 22). View the call to provide for your family with integrity

through the cross of Christ. Understand that there is honor in working hard and with honesty. "Anyone who does not provide for their relatives, and especially for their own household, has denied the faith and is worse than an unbeliever" (1 Tim. 5:8).

- "Whatever you do, work heartily, as for the Lord and not for men," (v. 23) View your call to give your all through the cross of Christ. Why? *Because He gave His all.* Give your all to being single, not seeking a mate! Give your all to be married and be willing to die for your spouse! Give your all to your kids and be willing to sow into their lives!

- "[K]nowing that from the Lord you will receive the inheritance as your reward. You are serving the Lord Christ" (v. 24). Please understand your real reward is *Christ*! This is sooooo important! Most of us slip into selfishness and forget how to serve others. Relationships are not "cross free" zones; you still have to carry one. Of course, this can be difficult when the other person won't carry his/hers, but you are only responsible for your cross. "For the wrongdoer will be paid back for the wrong he has done, and there is no partiality" (v. 25).

Jesus Is Enough **Questions:** In light of the preeminence of Christ, how should we view our important relationships with others? How should His Lordship impact your ability to love?

_____

_____

_____

_____

_____

_____

_____

_____

_____

_____

_____

_____

_____

_____

_____

GOD'S PURPOSE FOR YOU
AND HIS CHURCH

Read Ephesians 1:1–15

Is Jesus still enough for you?! We have spent the last few months reframing our perspectives on the kingdom of God, what true harvest means, and how to look at the Scriptures. Just reading the Word (instead of reading into it) has allowed us to arrive at an unselfish and uncomfortable place, as we've discovered that the kingdom is about Christ taking over the man rather than the Christian taking over the marketplace.

However, I believe our refocus on the core truths of the Word will help us to live and minister with new levels of power because we are effectively moving ourselves (our ambitions, our wants, our desires) out of the way and in their place inserting the will of God. We have starved ourselves of the fast food of what I call "Systematic Blessing Theology," and we are eating healthy meals. We are getting stronger in the faith because we have decided to embrace the real Christianity. So, I believe that we can now begin to embrace and execute what every biblical church is truly here for:

1. To reach, teach, and release hurting people through the power of Jesus Christ.
2. To help those same people discover life at Calvary (as it is presented in the Scriptures, not what we want it to be).
3. To present to our area and beyond a model of Christian integrity in the way we communicate Scripture, conduct our lives, manage our money, and walk in love with each other.
4. To penetrate culture and present Christ in fresh and innovative ways.
5. To fly a standard of biblical fidelity and to equip believers to share their faith.

Let's dig in. As we will see as we press into Ephesians, God sets the vision standard high for His church. In this book, he declares a new way of thinking and living in Christ.

He casts big vision for the way our lives should be lived, and he sets big goals for us, including:

- a vision of evangelism and good works
- a vision of racial unity and reconciliation
- a vision for a healthy church
- a vision for intentional living
- a vision for a healthy home
- a vision for success in spiritual warfare

But first, He does what we've been learning all year. He sets in stone your purpose and that of the church: the glory of Christ Jesus. Unlike other epistles, Ephesians was not written to combat heresy or error; rather, it was written to expand the kingdom understanding of its readers and the comprehension of God's purposes. Let's examine the purpose that we find in our text, Ephesians 1:1–15.

God wants us to know that:

1. We are blessed in Christ! (v. 3)

    - With every spiritual blessing in the heavenly places! Haven't we been here before?
    - When our lives shift from idolizing the temporal, it's amazing how much kingdom stuff you can get done!

2. We are chosen in Christ! (v. 4)

    - If you are willing to come to Christ, you are chosen. You are chosen to be holy and intimate with Christ.
    - The "chosen" must choose to walk in His purpose and blessings.

3. We are adopted in Christ! (v. 5)

    - We had no legal right to His estate, yet despite our sin, now we do.
    - Indeed we have the riches now simply because of our adoption!

4. We are redeemed in Christ! (v. 7)

    - Our redemption is through His blood and at His expense.
    - Why doesn't this reality have a greater impact on our decision making?
    - We are given "lavish" grace in Christ! (v8)

- "Lavish" is a term indicating passion and extravagance. Other versions may say, "abundant."
- God lavished his redemption and lavished his forgiveness upon us.
- We see God lavishing his grace in us by way of wisdom and insight. As a result, we are stewards over these mysteries in Christ (v. 9).

Based on this knowledge and all of these "real" blessings, God has purposed the church to:

1. Unify all things in Christ (v. 10)

    This is the great purpose and goal of the church. At His second coming (the "fulfillment or fullness of times"), this will be ultimately fulfilled. However, our job *now* is to take ground for the kingdom through our living and the way we teach others to live. Paul gives us what this looks like:

    a. Preaching to every person the mystery that has been revealed: forgiveness of sins and eternal life in Christ Jesus. (vv. 7–9)
    b. Teaching every person how to be "holy and blameless" (v. 4)
    c. A releasing of every person into the fullness of "every spiritual blessing in Christ" (v. 3)

    We know what Paul means by "every," when placed in the context of the Great Commission, and God's continuing plan to "unify" all things under Christ. (v10)

2. Live for His plan and in His will for "the praise of His glory." (vv. 11, 12)

    Paul begins to describe the mercy that both Jews and Gentiles who responded to Christ's call received. He then gives the reason for this call, which is the glory of God. You *must* understand that your daily response to Christ is your primary way of giving Him this glory. That is why *how* you live and *what* you think are *so critical*! That is why the "in Him" cannot be *part* of your life but must be your *whole* life! We have the ultimate inheritance in Christ! We should live each day as if we understood this! The highest form of glorifying Him is how we choose to live rather than what we say. He ensures everything conforms to the counsel of His will. (cf. Romans 8:28–30)

3. Courageously preach "the gospel of salvation." (vv. 13, 14)

    Regardless of race, when people respond to the "Word of truth" they demonstrate that they were also chosen. Furthermore, all believers are "sealed" by the Holy Spirit. It was critical that the world knew that both Jew and Gentile had received the same gift of Christ and the same Spirit (cf. Acts 19:1–6). What does this mean for us? It means that we are all the same in Christ. Race or gender means nothing in a spiritual sense. Amazingly, the Holy Spirit's presence guarantees us even more spiritual blessings in the resurrection! (v. 14)

By the way, fear is also conquered since we have been "sealed!" What is there to be afraid of now?

4. Walk in His purpose until our death or until He comes! (v. 14)

Again, His purpose is the *glory and headship of Christ*. We execute His purpose when we worship and preach Christ and love Him through our living. This passage says the Holy Spirit is our deposit until the redemption. "But aren't we already redeemed?" Yes and no.

Spiritually, we are righteous before God. Our position with God is no longer unrighteous but righteous. *Practically*, we still sin. In the resurrection, no trace of sin will remain in us. Neither our Spirits (which are already saved) nor our bodies (which certainly are not saved) will have any trace of sin. Only in the resurrection will our sin nature be fully dealt with.

Jesus in Enough Questions: How has your life started to reflect unity in Christ? Can you see that the sum of all things is about Christ? Is all this Christ stuff starting to get on your nerves?! Seriously, write out a few thoughts on your new or adjusted understanding of life's purpose, and that of the church.

_____

_____

_____

_____

_____

_____

_____

_____

_____

_____

_____

_____

_____

LESSON
20

PAUSING TO PRAY

Read Ephesians 1:15–23

Let's pause for prayer. The apostle Paul demonstrates a true shepherd's heart as he explains his prayers for the Ephesian church. He desperately wanted the saints at Ephesus to be focused on Christ at all costs. Begin to lay before God and pray these kinds of prayers for others. Specifically:

1. Pray that those you know would have an increased faith in Christ and a love for His people (v. 15).
2. Pray that those you know might have a "spirit of wisdom" and revelation to know the true Christ and true kingdom (v. 17).
3. Pray that saints everywhere would have enlightened eyes to know the real "hope" of Christ's inheritance: eternal life (v. 18).
4. Pray that those you know would walk in the power that raised Christ from the dead, so that they might live a resurrected life, "according to the power of his great might" (vv. 19, 20).
5. Pray they would be willing to walk under the headship and under the authority of Christ in their actions, thoughts, and heart (vv. 21–23).

Jesus Is Enough **Prayers:** List whom you are praying for, what you prayed, and how you felt as you were praying. Please note: this prayer time should not be centered on you. Part of learning that Christ is enough is learning how to focus outward; shifting one's heart from "me" to "Him," and through Him, to others.

_____

_____

_____

_____

_____

LESSON
21

THANKING GOD FOR HIS MERCY!

Read Ephesians 2:1–3

For your consideration during this lesson, here are some things to remember about Ephesians:

- It was written by Paul while he was imprisoned in Rome.
- As a circular letter, it was written to expand the kingdom perspective of its readers.
- It casts great vision for the plan of God for the church in chapter 1 and details how that vision should look in the rest of the chapters.
- With the vision cast in chapter 1, Paul begins laying out the sort of foundational plans the church should be pursuing. *This starts with an appreciation for where we are in Christ versus where we would be without Him!*

I'm convinced that a vast majority of church going Christians take their salvation for granted. In my opinion, the common culture based preaching that kingdom life is about gathering stuff and getting circumstantial blessings has led to this sad consequence. Remember, if you have placed your faith in Christ Jesus, you are "blessed in the heavenly realms with every spiritual blessing in Christ" (Eph. 1:3).

Thoughts from the text:

Understand that sin separates (v. 1).

The word *sin* literally means, "to miss the mark." God is perfect in holiness and hates sin (Ps. 18:30; 99:5; Prov. 6:16–19). Therefore, we needed a Savior because our sins kept us from God. The definition of "death" (in the ultimate sense) is separation from God. Understanding our sin in relation to our salvation should bring exuberant praise to our Lord. Why don't we rejoice in this wondrous miracle? Why isn't the promise of Christ enough?

Our old, non-harvest lives were ruled by Satan's power (v. 2).

"In which you once walked" or "used to live" (NIV) suggests we don't live that way anymore! Following the ways of the world *is to follow the ruler of the kingdom of the air*! Whoa! Have we let the world's pursuits influence how we interpret Scripture? "*Do not love the world or the things in the world. If anyone loves the world, the love of the Father is not in him. For all that is in the world—the desires of the flesh and the desires of the eyes and pride of life—is not from the Father but is from the world. And the world is passing away along with its desires, but whoever does the will of God abides forever.*" (1 John 2:15–17). If the world is pursuing *p*rosperity, if the world is pursing *p*ersonal recognition, if the world is pursuing *p*ower, if the world is pursuing *p*leasure and ease, what should *we* be pursuing? Maybe the *p*urpose of God?

We are all in the same boat: former slaves to sin (v. 3)

Recognizing this should prevent the holier than thou prideful spirit and should cause a true sense of appreciation for the grace and mercy of Jesus. The assumption is that those of us walking in the harvest of God's mercy have left our old life and cravings behind to love Christ daily. We are truly battling with our sinful nature daily. Make no mistake: it *is* a battle. Take a moment to read Romans 7:14–25 and Galatians 5:13–26. The reality is that we deserve death for our sins. Sadly, most of us walk around under the mercy/grace covering of Christ (which was purchased with His blood) with a deep sense of cultural entitlement and an overwhelming lack of real appreciation for the cross. Even as we confess sins and ask for forgiveness, we don't really make the mental and emotional connection that without the blood of Jesus, *just one little sin* is enough to condemn us to an eternity without Christ. Where is our appreciation for what He has done? Where is the awe, the sense of being overwhelmed by His mercy, the joyful thankfulness that should cause us to explode in worship, service, giving, evangelism, and love-based holiness?

Could it be that connecting the cross with cash (the sacrifice with stuff; the miracle with materialism, the promise with purchase power) has diluted our gratitude for the real kingdom abundance Christ promised? Could it be?

Jesus Is Enough **Questions:** How do you really feel about the mercy of God and its connection to your salvation? Does your life demonstrate a deep, passionate thankfulness for simply being saved? Does your worship reflect God's mercy? Does your giving? Does your evangelism and discipleship?

_____

_____

_____

_____

_____

_____

_____

_____

_____

LESSON
22

THANKING GOD FOR HIS SALVATION

When I was growing up, we sang a song in church that said, "Glad to be in God's service, glad to be in God's service, glad to be in God's service … one more time. He didn't have to let me live, He didn't have to let me live. Glad to be in God's service, one more time." I didn't know it then, but the saints were simply expressing their joy in the salvation of God. They were singing about the simple but profound privilege of serving Him joyfully.

Read Ephesians 2:4–10

My friends, here are just a few simple, uncomplicated thoughts for you during this lesson. God loves you and shows it. Look at what Paul said to the church at Rome.

> [B]ut God shows his love for us in that while we were still sinners, Christ died for us. Since, therefore, we have now been justified by his blood, much more shall we be saved by him from the wrath of God. For if while we were enemies we were reconciled to God by the death of his Son, much more, now that we are reconciled, shall we be saved by his life. More than that, we also rejoice in God through our Lord Jesus Christ, through whom we have now received reconciliation." (Rom. 5:8–11)

So given our recaptured focus on Christ alone, let's simply rejoice in Him and in His salvation. Everything else pales in comparison to the gift of God in Christ Jesus— eternal life.

"For the wages of sin is death, but the free gift of God is eternal life in Christ Jesus our Lord." (Rom. 6:23)

Thoughts to meditate on:

1. Despite deserving death, God chose to give us life! (v. 4)

   My challenge to you is to consider what you have learned from the lessons thus far and really think through the ramifications of this statement. The fuel of the Christian's joy is the hope of his salvation. This joy is even greater when we consider from the context how completely undeserving we actually are! Thank you, Jesus!

2. God's motive for granting us life is love! (v. 4)

   As a matter of fact, God's motive for His entire redemptive plan is love as John 3:16 illustrates. Remember, "God is love" (1 John 4:8), so giving, grace, and mercy are part of His character. Notice the passion in the phrase: "his great love for us." His love for us is pure, with no strings attached. He loves us not for what we can do for Him, but for who we are in Him. Should we do any differently?

3. We walk daily in the "riches" of God's love! (vv. 4, 5)

   How? His mercy stayed His righteous hand, even when we were in sin. His grace offered us salvation so we could begin again! We are incapable of even working our way into God's holy presence. So God had to provide the way through His own blood. Bless the Lord! Getting excited yet?

4. Consider the daily implications of "being seated with Christ!" (vv. 6, 7)

   Now, we have the privilege of being intimate with Him in prayer, worship, service, mind, and heart. In the coming ages, the limitations of our current relationship with Him will be stripped away, and the full expression of His kindness will be manifest. This is the joy of the Christian life: Christ!

5. Salvation is a gift from God! (vv. 8, 9)

   The worldly notion of standing up, taking charge, making it happen, and making your dreams come true are secular mind-sets that must be vetted through verses like this.

   Bragging about what you have and boldly claiming what you want are not actions that are congruent with Scripture. Remember, God prizes humility and hates pride (cf. 1 Pet. 5:5). Our salvation by grace through faith alone is a constant reminder that "without Him, we can do nothing." (John 15:5)

6. The restoration of "salvation joy" should result in God's purpose in our lives. (v. 10)

We are all called to good works, as God defines "good." The best rewards for the works we do are spiritual and heavenly in nature. We should make the connection between the right motive for joy (Jesus is enough) and the expression of the real joy he promised. If we are His workmanship, we are created to work like Him.

With the right perspective about God and toward His salvation, we should naturally want to give because He gave, love because He loves, bless because He blesses, forgive because He forgives, serve because He served us, and worship because He is worthy. This should be the natural response of those who truly understand salvation.

Jesus Is Enough Questions: Is God worthy of your worship and praise? How is He worthy to you, given what you have learned? Tell Him below.

_____

_____

_____

_____

_____

_____

_____

_____

_____

_____

_____

_____

_____

_____

_____

```
┌─────────────────┐
│     LESSON      │
│       23        │
└─────────────────┘
```

ONE IN CHRIST

Part of the blessing of *Jesus Is Enough* is embracing the Spirit's work in our understanding of "oneness." One of the greatest blessings of kingdom life on earth is the fact that we are in a "body"; we are a "house"; we are an "army." When Christ becomes enough, this reality begins to mean more than it ever has for the Christian.

Read Ephesians 2:11–22 and Ephesians chapter 3

Thoughts to meditate on:

1. Consider the words *separated*, *alienated*, and *strangers* in this context. (vv. 11, 12):

    Paul is talking to people who by virtue of their birth (or race) were unable to connect with God. He is beginning to paint the picture of bringing all things under the unity of Christ. This unification includes Jew and Gentile, and by extension, all races, all ages, and socio-economic brackets. What are we doing as a church and as individuals to foster separation, exclusion, and the discomfort of being "foreigner?" Do we see this in our homes, churches, or jobs? Jesus said, "You're blessed when you can show people how to cooperate instead of compete or fight. That's when you discover who you really are, and your place in God's family." (Matt. 5:9 MSG) We know that both the Word and Christ Himself will sometimes cause division; but the task of the believer is to stand strong on our biblical convictions *and* unite people to each other and to Christ. Only the Holy Spirit can do this!

    In a very real way, we believers are the Jews (or true Israel), and those without Christ are Gentiles. What are you doing to give them hope? (vv. 12, 13)

    "Gentiles" are separated from Christ, excluded from the kingdom, and without hope. They are all around us right now. Since every believer "has been brought near by the blood of Christ," we have been given "the ministry of reconciliation." (2 Cor. 5:19)

```
```

2. Christ Himself is our peace! (vv. 14–18)

Just look at the vision of unity and joy these verses cast! True peace only flows from Christ, and that peace is supposed to be ours. All race barriers are destroyed in Christ Jesus! No, I'm not naïve; I just believe! Here's why:

   a. The standards of the Law have been superseded by blood-bought grace! It is the cross that unites us and reconciles us all to God. Therefore, the cross enables us to forgive each other.
   b. We all have one Spirit. Therefore, we are brothers and sisters in the eternal sense!
   c. The church should reflect this "one new humanity:" all races and ages with the same heart, mind, love, and vision.

3. We are no longer on the outside looking in! (v. 19)

Everything we do as a church must reflect this reality. Reading this, I was so convicted. I can look around us and see walls we have inadvertently put up that say "If you are not like us in race, style, or manner you are not welcome." Those walls must come down immediately. Are you willing to change to let your life reflect verse 19?

4. Jesus Christ is the chief cornerstone! (v. 20)

I love this song that Paul Oakley wrote:

   It's all about you, Jesus.
   And all this is for you,
   For your glory and your fame.
   It's not about me,
   As if you should do things my way.
   You alone are God and I surrender,
   To your way.
   ("Jesus Lover Of My Soul")

He is truly enough, and the one that enables us to forgive, drop our human prejudices, and live in the kingdom of God.

5. When Christ is the focus, the kingdom moves with unstoppable momentum! (vv. 21, 22)

- When it is He and not you, we are joined together.
- When it is He and not you, we rise.
- When it is He and not you, we can walk in holiness.
- When it is He and not you, we are built up in unity.
- When it is He and not you, we experience the fullness of the Holy Spirit.
- At any point, if you move in front of Him, these blessings are nullified.
- Not appreciating the price He paid for our reconciliation promotes self.

As we consider our unity in Christ ... that such a vision carries a price:

I became a servant of this gospel by the gift of God's grace given me through the working of his power. Although I am less than the least of all the Lord's people, this grace was given me: to preach to the Gentiles the boundless riches of Christ, and to make plain to everyone the administration of this mystery, which for ages past was kept hidden in God, who created all things. His intent was that now, through the church, the manifold wisdom of God should be made known to the rulers and authorities in the heavenly realms, according to his eternal purpose that he accomplished in Christ Jesus our Lord. In him and through faith in him we may approach God with freedom and confidence. I ask you, therefore, not to be discouraged because of my sufferings for you, which are your glory. (Eph. 3:7–13)

1. Service: Paul gave up all to follow Christ. (Eph. 3:7)
2. Servanthood: The "great apostle" considered himself less than everyone else. (Eph. 3:8)
3. Soldiering: Standing against spiritual "rulers and authorities" with the truth of the gospel is dangerous work. (Eph. 3:10)
4. Suffering: considered by Paul to be "glory" for the church. Wow. (Eph. 3:13)

A Prayer for the church:

Father, we ask that ...

1. We believers would realize we have the same family name and should therefore fight for family unity.
2. You would strengthen us in our hearts, minds, and spirit with whom Jesus is and that He alone is our hope, our love, and our joy.
3. We in our families and in our church would be "rooted [meaning it goes deep] and established [implying it goes wide]" in love, because, "Love never gives up. Love cares more for others than for self. Love doesn't want what it doesn't have. Love doesn't strut, doesn't have a swelled head, doesn't force itself on others, isn't always 'me first,' doesn't fly off the handle, doesn't keep

score of the sins of others, doesn't revel when others grovel, takes pleasure in the flowering of truth, puts up with anything, trusts God always, always looks for the best, never looks back, but keeps going to the end. Love never dies … (1 Cor. 13:4–8, MSG).

4. We might gain a greater understanding of your love and sacrifice, and allow that understanding to empower our love for others, better decisions, contentment, and peace in our lives.

5. We would never put what You can do in our lives before Your glory in our lives. We ask You to do great things through us, but only to the extent that You receive the glory and not us.

In Jesus' name … Amen.

Jesus Is Enough Questions: *What can you do to change how divided we all seem to be in Christ? Do you need to get before God so you can see Christians of all races, ages, and socio-economic backgrounds as your true brothers and sisters in the Lord? What are you praying on behalf of God's holy church?*

_____

_____

_____

_____

_____

_____

_____

_____

_____

_____

_____

_____

_____

_____

_____

LESSON
24

WALKING IN UNITY!

In the last lesson, Paul's vision for the church, personal willingness to sacrifice, and overall prayer for the local church in Ephesians chapters 2 and 3 edified and challenged us. In this lesson, Paul shifts gears. Based on the huge vision cast in the first three chapters of Ephesians, he now throws out a huge challenge. In simple terms, he says, *"be mature!"* Oh how we need this in our modern church culture! It's time to grow up in the Lord!

Read Ephesians 4:1–6

Thoughts from the text:

1. We first begin with a question. Why did Paul frame his prisoner status as a place of authority to issue the call? (v. 1)

   Certainly, any person in prison doesn't hold power or authority. However, it is almost as if he is asking, "Since I've given up my physical freedom for His sake, what are you willing to give up?" This gets to the heart of our teaching emphasis in this book. Instead of seeing Christianity as the means by which we get all we want on earth, should we instead see serving Christ as living in a sacrificial manner so He gets what He wants on earth?

2. We must live in a manner worthy of Christ. (v. 1)

   This call is not about a list of rules but rather a love of the Redeemer. Although he lists quite a few things throughout the rest of the book that would demonstrate this high level of living, the overall emphasis is on a change of the heart toward Christ. Paul says to the Colossians, "We have not ceased to pray for you, asking that you may be filled with the knowledge of his will in all spiritual wisdom and understanding, so as to walk in a manner worthy of the Lord, fully pleasing to him, bearing fruit in every good work and increasing in the knowledge of God" (Col. 1:9–10). Walking worthy of Christ begins with the heart. We transform from selfishness to sacrifice, me first to maturity, and from the winds of culture to the will of Christ.

3. "Living worthy" is less about what you achieve and more about how you adore. (v. 2)

Again, Christ is concerned about your heart. That is where His current kingdom does its primary work and how His current kingdom expands and grows. Humility, gentleness, patience, and love are heart issues first, and translate into Christ honoring actions. Jesus always wants to get to the heart of the issue: "But what comes out of the mouth proceeds from the heart, and this defiles a person. For out of the heart come evil thoughts, murder, adultery, sexual immorality, theft, false witness, slander. These are what defile a person. But to eat with unwashed hands does not defile anyone" (Matt. 15:18–20).

4. Our unity flows from our focus on the Spirit. (v. 3)

Ephesians 4:3, NIV says, "Make every effort to keep the unity of the Spirit," while ESV says, "eager to maintain the unity of the Spirit." What do "make every effort" and "[be] eager to maintain," mean to you? Here is a difficult truth: where the Spirit is given reign, there should be unity. There should be unity in our marriages, churches, leadership team, etc. Here are a few things a surrendered Spirit will naturally produce with respect to unity: quick repentance, a refusal to hold a grudge, a spirit of giving, and a willingness to place others first, and a refusal to gossip.

5. If we can all focus on the one hope that is in Christ alone, we can walk in the power of unity. (v. 4)

Our calling is "to one hope." Biblically, that one hope is the hope of eternal life in Jesus Christ. Our focus on this hope should naturally bring unity in the body by the Spirit. Jesus and His salvation power become enough for us so that there is no longer any need to fuss, fight, and covet! When Jesus is enough, you will be released to love and be set free from the bondage of self.

6. If we can put our faith in the one Lord, we can walk in the power of unity. (v. 5)

This seems simple because it is! Jesus is our one Lord! Our one faith rests in Jesus being the Son of God and God the son. Identification with the one Savior through baptism demonstrates our unity with the body.

7. If we understand that our one God is enough, we can walk in the power of unity. (v. 6)

Jesus is over all, completely sovereign and omnipotent. He works through each believer to accomplish His loving purpose. Jesus is in each believer and is ready to help each of us walk in His love toward each other. If Jesus is truly over all in our lives, unity will naturally flow from us.

A few more thoughts on unity:

- Stop seeing Christian disunity as normal; dream big!
- Stop seeing serving others as a chore; love big!
- Stop seeing other believers as a liability; trust big!
- Stop seeing the tongue as a small thing; speak big!
- Stop seeing the church as a bunch of hypocrites; connect big!

Jesus Is Enough **Questions:** What do you have to change to "walk in a manner worthy" of the calling? Whom do you need to be more patient with? Are you eager to maintain peace? What does the phrase, "one Lord, one faith, one baptism" mean to you?

_____

_____

_____

_____

_____

_____

_____

_____

_____

_____

_____

_____

_____

_____

EQUIPPED FOR SERVICE

In the previous lesson, we saw a shift in Ephesians. After casting huge kingdom vision in the first three chapters, Paul now throws out a huge calling. In simple terms, he exclaims, "Be mature!" I think this transition in the text hits the church square between the eyes. It's now time for us to walk in the Word we've been given. It's time to grow up in the Lord, and nothing measures maturity like our willingness to lovingly and gracefully serve others. I've come to the conclusion that without a heart for service, there can be no reaching, teaching, and releasing of hurting people. At the heart of serving is a willingness to give selflessly. Reaching people will required your time, teaching people will require your talent and releasing people will require your treasure. At the heart of this lesson text is the call for leaders to equip God's people to serve by giving all three.

Read Ephesians 4:7–16

Thoughts from the text:

1. For the sake of serving others, Christ gives us grace. (v. 7)

   God's divine favor, or grace, is needed not only to "live a life worthy of the calling," but also to help us understand and embrace the gifts He's given to the body. In Romans 12:5–6, Paul equates spiritual gifts with grace. In other words, we are saved to serve and we are given to give. As we will see, in addition to individual gifts, He also gave the gifts of different kinds of leaders to His church.

2. For the sake of serving others, Christ modeled sacrifice. (vv. 8–10)

   The imagery here is of a conquering king returning to his throne after having defeated his enemies, who are trailing behind him in humiliation. To say that these verses teach that Christ descended into Hell, took the keys, and freed "captives" from Abraham's bosom and leads them home (which is a common interpretation) misses the point of the verse and the chapter. "Captives" more naturally refer to the spiritual enemies defeated by His brutal crucifixion and His glorious resurrection. The point here is that the crucified "criminal" became the conquering king and now gives "gifts" to his body to maintain his victory!

3. For the sake of serving others, Christ put human "gifts" into the body. (v. 11)

Rather than becoming hung up on titles, consider the context: Christ loves the church enough to appoint people to care for it. Therefore, those who lead should love as He loved. Here's how:

    a) When a leader considers Christ's descent, it should cause deep humility and integrity. Why? Because "[Christ] emptied himself, by taking the form of a servant, being born in the likeness of men. And being found in human form, he humbled himself by becoming obedient to the point of death, even death on a cross." (Phil. 2:7–8)

    b) When a leader considers Christ's ascension, it should cause a sense of overwhelming awe and responsibility. Rather than trying to outrank each other, the leader should be busy serving and modeling Christlike attributes.

4. For the sake of serving others, Christ calls leaders to equip the church. (vv. 12, 13)

In these verses, the frame of reference for the leader is to equip for service. Paul's charge was to equip the Saints to work in ministry and build up the body. I wonder what would happen if we viewed all we are taught through the eyes of Jesus. I wonder what would happen if each sermon had a threefold, interconnected purpose in our hearts: to give Him glory, to grow in Him and to share Him with others. I wonder what would happen if we grew more unified around Christ alone, became well versed in doctrine, and grew in the character of Jesus.

5. In service to others, Christ calls leaders (those who are mature) to facilitate the benefits of this sort of growth and maturity. In essence, the leader is called to

- teach them (v. 14);
- protect them (v. 14);
- correct them in love (v. 15);
- facilitate their growth in Him (v. 15);
- keep their focus on Him (v. 16); and
- get everyone involved in His work (v. 16).

Jesus Is Enough **Questions:** In your sphere of influence, there are people right now that you are equipped to serve. The service will likely be long and difficult. You might have to feed or clothe them. You might have to read and study to answer their questions. You might have to walk with them through painful issues for months or years. There will be a temptation to back away to pursue personal comforts. How will you handle this?

_____
_____
_____
_____
_____
_____
_____
_____
_____
_____
_____
_____
_____

GROWING IN MENTAL STRENGTH

During this lesson, we will discuss one of the key battlegrounds in the maturity of every Christian. This area will often determine how successful you will be in achieving God's purpose for your life. This area is your mind. The Bible talks often about the spirit, soul, heart, and mind of man. These terms are often used interchangeably, so we aren't trying to be very dogmatic on how separate the spirit and soul are. However, for the purposes of this lesson, let's break it down this way:

- The spirit of man is who he is.
- The soul of man is where he decides.
- The body of man is where he acts.

Here is a profound mystery: As a Christian, your spirit (who you truly are; that inner part of you that will go to be with the Lord) *is* saved, your mind (that inner part of you still maturing through the application of the Word) is *being* saved, and your body (the outer man, and the part of you that must be crucified daily) *will be* saved! So, if you ever feel like you have two or three people fighting inside you … you do!

Key point: After your salvation, there isn't much you can do with your Spirit. Until the resurrection, there isn't much you can do with your body either. So, where does true maturity happen? You guessed it … in your mind (heart, intellect, and seat of emotions).

The word for *minds* in Ephesians 4:17 is the word *nous*. It means "the seat of reflective consciousness; one's understanding and ability to determine, or one's intellect." Your spirit is willing to serve God; your body is not. The mature mind wants to serve God but must constantly be on alert for immaturity. Below is a quick biblical survey of the "mind"

- "For out of the *heart* come evil *thoughts*, murder, adultery, sexual immorality, theft, false witness, slander." (Matt. 15:19)
- "And he said to him, "You shall love the Lord your God with all your heart and with all your soul and with all your *mind*." (Matt. 22:37)
- "Thanks be to God through Jesus Christ our Lord! So then, I myself serve the law of God with my *mind*, but with my flesh I serve the law of sin." (Rom. 7:25)
- "For the *mind* that is set on the flesh is hostile to God, for it does not submit to God's law; indeed, it cannot. Those who are in the flesh cannot please God." (Rom. 8:7–8)
- "Do not be conformed to this world, but be transformed by the renewal of your *mind*, that by testing you may discern what is the will of God, what is good and acceptable and perfect." (Rom. 12:2)
- "Brothers, do not be children in your *thinking*. Be infants in evil, but in your *thinking* be mature." (1 Cor. 14:20)
- "And the peace of God, which surpasses all understanding, will guard your *hearts* and your *minds* in Christ Jesus. Finally, brothers, whatever is true, whatever is honorable, whatever is just, whatever is pure, whatever is lovely, whatever is commendable, if there is any excellence, if there is anything worthy of praise, *think* about these things." (Phil. 4:7–8)

Read Ephesians 4:17–24

Thoughts from the text:

1. Your thinking affects your living (v. 17)

   Note first that Paul doesn't attack the Ephesian's behavior; he attacks their thinking. As we have seen, your behavior is influenced by the heart and mind. I once told my congregants, "Life is a series of interconnected choices. The quickest way to God's purpose is to make the right decisions." This is so true. A mature mind embraces personal responsibility in making holy, integrity based choices.

2. A low understanding of God results in low living in God (v. 18)

   The command to seek God in our understanding is replete through the Bible, especially in Proverbs. This understanding results in a Christ-based mentality, without which we suffer the pains of daily mediocrity. The darker your understanding, the lower you live. So, what is living in God? Purpose, joy, peace, contentment, intimacy, discipling others, and much more!

3. Ignorance is not always innocent (v. 18)

Sometimes, ignorance comes from stubbornness. It's not that we don't know but sometimes, we simply don't want to know. We must not use ignorance as a shield or an excuse to continue misbehaviors we like. If we do, it leads to my next point …

4. Refusing to mature mentally and emotionally results in desensitization (v. 19)

This verse sums up much of the culture, and much of the church. Sadly, this is not only a reality but also a reality that we celebrate. The willingness to live "in the futility" of immature thinking has resulted in an approval and even a promotion of things God hates in our society such as:

- greed and materialism
- sexual sin and perversion
- pride and egotism
- grudge holding and unforgiveness
- the systematic tearing down of the traditional family unit

5. Old living means old problems; new living means new kingdom opportunities (vv. 20–24)

The best opportunities are in Jesus because the best opportunity **is** Jesus. Jesus is the only way to obtain the new self-created after the likeness of God. If you have truly put on the new self, you will naturally begin to view life like Christ, give like Christ and love like Christ.

Jesus Is Enough **Questions:** What are you doing daily to be "renewed in the spirit of your mind?" Do you have any "old self" stuff that needs to be put off today? Putting it bluntly, how is your walk and where are your thoughts normally directed?

_____

_____

_____

_____

_____

_____

_____

_____

_____

_____

_____

_____

_____

GROWING IN RIGHT BEHAVIORS

Read Ephesians 4:25–32

This lesson text indicates that the maturation of both our kingdom perspective and mental focus should produce some shifts in our behaviors. These behavior changes are key to the original vision presented in chapter 1 of this epistle:

- Unify all things in Christ! This is the great purpose and goal of the church!
- Live for His plan and in His will for "the praise of His glory."
- Courageously preach "the Gospel of salvation."
- Walk in His purpose (the glory and headship of Christ) until our death or until He comes!

Thoughts from the text:

In our text, Paul lists a few growth areas that will be evident after putting on the new self that is created in the likeness of God. We must:

1. Grow in courageous honesty (v. 25)

   Paul is referencing any kind of lying, deceit or dishonesty. However, many of us present and/or live with a false image of who we really are. We also allow those we say we love to do the same. All of this is dishonest. How much love and integrity would it take you to simply be truthful with your neighbor?

2. Grow in difficult reconciliation (vv. 26, 27)

   This verse essentially gives us a time limit on how long we should stay in an unrepentant condition. No more than twenty-four hours, max! It takes maturity to be the first one to repent, but it must be done if you claim to have a renewed mind in

Christ. We've all seen what happens when there is no forgiveness over long periods of time. This is nothing but satanic influence to create disunity.

3. Grow in both work effort and work ethic (v. 28)

This is the simple call for an honest day's work for an honest day's pay. Not only is this honesty toward the employer but it honors God. In addition, Paul states that working with your hands allows you to share with those in need. God gives us the ability to gain wealth for the sake of His love-based covenant with us. (Deut. 8:18)

4. Grow in giving (v. 28)

Put simply, we are "blessed to be a blessing." We are stewards of God's resources and should prepare ourselves to be a blessing to others. Proverbs 21:26 teaches that it is the righteous who give and withhold nothing. Increase your giving toward others and watch your growth!

5. Grow in verbal encouragement (v. 29)

Here is the true power of the tongue. Our words are not to create reality or shape our universe, as new agers believe. Rather, they are for creating relationships. Most people (Christians included) are *starving* for verbal validation. Breathe in this verse, and for the rest of the year, build others up with your words and watch what happens!

6. Grow in Spirit-pleasing activities (vv. 30–32)

   - Instead of getting bitter, we must learn to get better.
   - Instead of walking in anger, we must worship in adoration.
   - Instead of fighting, we must forgive.
   - Instead of slandering, we must serve.

Verse 32, special mention:

This verse is the key to so much progress in so many of the situations you are currently dealing with. It takes a mature mind and a loving heart to walk consistently in this mandate. Let us, as Christians, keep in mind that it was compassion and an overwhelming desire to forgive that caused Christ to come in the flesh. Let's follow His example!

***Jesus Is Enough* Questions:** Have you put away anything false? Are you keeping short accounts with God and others? Are there any unguarded places in your life where the Devil can get his foot in? Are you building others up with your words? Are you living a life of truth-filled kindness? Write your honest thoughts below:

_____

_____

_____

_____

_____

_____

_____

_____

_____

_____

_____

_____

_____

_____

LESSON
28

EXPLORING SOME FAMILY FOUNDATIONS

Read Ephesians chapter 5

As we enter chapter 5, it is my conviction during this particular teaching to approach the entire chapter (and indeed, the rest of the book) from a "family is foundational" perspective. In other words, we are following Paul's pattern in this book by narrowing our perspective from the big picture (unifying all things) to the personal. Please note that since the beginning of chapter 4, Paul's tone shifted from vision casting and servanthood to an authoritative voice. These are not suggestions; these are commands. Why? *How can we walk in the vision cast so far if our homes and personal behaviors don't honor God?* Let's explore some *Family Foundations.*

Foundation 1: Christ-based Decisions (v. 1)

Here are three words that can change your family and your home forever: *"Follow God's example."* Truly embracing these three words will be a fortifying process that could change your home and generations to come. What if we prayed before we talked, bought, or fought? When Christ is the center of our marriage, our decisions will be Christ based. Therefore, conversations about money and parenting will never be issues. Imagine if our homes were like little churches. What if we became so committed to the Word that we wore our "Jesus" lenses all the time?

Foundation 2: Sacrificial Love (vv. 1, 2)

The first way we follow Him is a commitment to loving one another sacrificially. The word *walk* suggests a *lifestyle* of putting others before yourself. Most problems in the home flow from selfishness on somebody's part. That is the opposite of the love Jesus requires. When Christ loves, He gives. He laid down His life as a demonstration of the "greatest love." Jesus tell us in John 15:13 and 14 that there is no greater love than a man who lays down his life for his friends. Jesus then concludes by saying, we are his friends! What if everyone in the home said these words today: "I die to myself. How can I best serve you mom/dad/wife/husband?" The antidote to hostility in the family is humility. The opposite of lust (which is selfish by its very nature) is love.

Foundation 3: Purity (vv. 3–5)

Ouch, ouch, and *ouch!* By the standards of verses 3 and 4, how many of us need to just throw the TV out of the house?! Although we aren't the people depicted in verse 5 due to our salvation, participation in these sins is wrong. Regardless of what is popular or even fun, we must examine what we are willing to do to fortify our family's purity? What are we willing to give up? What are we willing to sacrifice?

Foundation 4: Truth (v. 6)

Even believers sometimes struggle with the concept of an absolute truth. To call something "wrong" smacks of being judgmental: a taboo in our politically correct society. The idea of truth being absolute is considered crazy talk in our culture. Stating that we have and know the truth is a major taboo in a politically correct society. Nevertheless, truth by its very nature means that there can only be one truth. Don't be deceived into thinking, "what's right for them is right for them and what's right for me is right for me." Unless we establish Christ's absolute rule and truth in our homes, we will continue to slide down the slippery slope of compromise. Your home will fail if it is founded on anything less that the truth of God's word. Consider the words of Jesus in Matthew 7:24–27:

> *Everyone then who hears these words of mine and does them will be like a wise man who built his house on the rock. And the rain fell, and the floods came, and the winds blew and beat on that house, but it did not fall, because it had been founded on the rock. And everyone who hears these words of mine and does not do them will be like a foolish man who built his house on the sand. And the rain fell, and the floods came, and the winds blew and beat against that house, and it fell, and great was the fall of it.*

Foundation 5: Separation (vv. 7–14)

This is a tough one. Society and culture teaches us to be inclusive at all costs. God's Word challenges us to welcome anyone into the family of Christ, but also to separate ourselves from those working against it (v. 7). At times, for our families' sake, we must have the courage to be labeled "intolerant" or "extreme." Sometimes, we even must be willing to draw the line for our children, who many times won't understand our fight for their purity. For the sake of "living in the light," we have to first expose and then remove the darkness. We must wake up to the darkness in our homes and embrace the light of Christ. Sadly, many Christians are so enamored with culture that these words fall on deaf ears, and their families will soon fall as well.

Foundation 6: Wisdom (vv. 15, 16)

If this isn't an urgent call for families, nothing is! How much biblical "care" do we inject into our family lives? Please don't miss the urgency in verse 16. This is not something to mull over. This is something to act on now! Wisdom involves the "fear of the Lord." After all, this is the beginning of wisdom (Ps. 111:10; Prov. 9:10). So any family that isn't "careful to live" by what God has said is building their house on sand. Wisdom also involves making decisions based upon principles; recognizing that unwise decisions have consequences; and using God's Word as a continual guide for life (many Christians do not consult the Word prior to making decisions). Based on Proverbs, a family committed to God's wisdom will:

1. Have protection from wicked men (Prov. 2:12)
2. Be saved from adultery and perversion. (Prov. 2:16)
3. Have direction and focus. (Prov. 5:1)
4. Experience long years of living well. (Prov. 9:11)
5. Experience less drama. (Prov. 13:10)
6. Have the patience to fortify their relationships. (Prov. 19:11)
7. Have a vision! (Prov. 24:3; 29:18)

Foundation 7: Operating in the will of God (v. 17)

A family must be committed to "biblical transformation" (Rom. 12:2) to know God's will. Here are some suggestions on how a family can fortify itself in God's will:

1. Study the Word together
2. Pray together
3. Get Godly counsel when needed
4. Look for and act on God's activity

Also consider this practical suggestion: when trying to determine God's will in any situation (especially in issues of timing), go to and obey the principles. In other words, *when you don't know what to do, do what you know to do.* You can never go wrong by obeying God's principles and amazingly, when we walk like this, timing always works itself out.

Foundation 8: Worship (vv. 18–20)

These verses literally give a blueprint for the sort of atmosphere that grows God-fearing children, produces joyful marriages, and encourages joy in singles. Let's break it down.

"And do not get drunk with wine for that is debauchery …" (v. 18)

This is not just a law against drunkenness; it's a call to a disciplined atmosphere. Debauchery is an indulgence in sensual pleasures. This is a call for all of us to live with self-control and to eliminate anything that moves our homes away from godliness. This kind of living is a part of worship.

"[B]ut be filled with the Spirit," (v. 18)

At its core, being "filled with the Spirit" is less about gifts and more about surrender. Surrender leads to the appropriate use in service. This is exactly what we miss in families. What if we taught our children to surrender totally to God as their gifts began to manifest? And what if we served each other with surrendered, Spirit-filled hearts? Wow! This kind of surrendered service is a part of our Spiritual worship.

"[A]ddressing one another in psalms and hymns and spiritual songs, singing and making melody to the Lord with your heart," (v. 19)

There is so much fortifying power in how we communicate to each other and to God. Our homes should reflect our commitment to let all things seen and heard give glory to God. Is your family involved in consistent family worship? Do you speak to each other in Psalms (i.e., giving praise to God in both what we say and how we say it)? Are you teaching your children the Word of God and songs of worship and praise?

"[G]iving thanks always and for everything to God the Father in the name of our Lord Jesus Christ," (v. 20)

This verse is about God's provision and His sovereignty. Giving thanks to God "for everything" means we realize that we control nothing. This should produce humility, peace, and thankfulness in every family member.

Foundation 9: Submission (v. 21)

Great families eventually understand something Jesus said: "You know that the rulers of the Gentiles lord it over them, and their great ones exercise authority over them. It shall not be so among you. But whoever would be great among you must be your servant, and whoever would be first among you must be your slave, even as the Son of Man came not to be served but to serve, and to give his life as a ransom for many." (Matt. 20:25–28) Having said that, it is critical to know that verse 21 ("submitting to one another out of reverence for Christ." [Eph. 5:21]) in *no way* mitigates against male headship. In fact, verse 21 describes the kind of "one another" submission that follows: wives to husbands, children to parents, and servants to masters. (Eph. 5:22–6:9) Within the context of God-ordained authority in the home (Christ, husband-dad, wife-mom, children), there is room for all to serve one another in love.

Jesus Is Enough Questions: How can your family walk in the blessings of Ephesians 5 in a more profound way? Take a moment and jot down a family plan. Then share it with your spouse and/or older children. Pray it through and change your home!

LESSON
29

THE KEY TO THE HOME IS CHRIST!

Read Ephesians 5:22–33; 6:1–4:

Although these verses primarily deal with married people, there are lessons here for married, single, and parents. Instead of focusing on authority and role within this lesson, I feel led to go to the foundational area that precede authority and even service: Christ. We often want to jump to authority and role in the home ("submit," "head of," "obey," etc.), and we miss laying the proper foundation. We all tend to do this from time to time. For example, I once asked my church to give extra money for our building before I adequately trained them in stewardship. I ran into "foundational" issues. We weren't healthy enough to give the way we wanted. Dave Ramsey's Momentum was an effort to build the proper foundation.[1] Likewise, families run into trouble when they jump to the "organizational chart" before the mission has been defined. Likewise, the family is no different. Its primary mission is Christ. Our approach in this lesson will be to learn the mind-set and heart of these phrases:

- "[O]ut of reverence for *Christ*" (v. 21)
- "[A]s you do the *Lord*" (v. 22)
- "[L]ove … as *Christ* loved … and gave Himself up" (v. 25)
- "This is … about *Christ* and the church." (v. 32)
- "[T]raining and instruction of the *Lord*" (Eph. 6:4)

Lessons and Heart:

1. The key to a harvest in the home is Christ.

- Jesus must be *enough* in every home. He must be the center of every home.
- He must be the foundational point of every marriage, single person, and parental relationship.

2. For all: There can be no mutual submission unless Christ is revered.

- To "revere" means to regard with the deepest respect, deference, and esteem. *Revere* suggests, "awe coupled with profound honor." (American Heritage Dictionary)
- *It's impossible to view another this way without first seeing Christ this way. This is a huge point. Get this!*

3. For wives: Submission cannot be accomplished and consistent unless the first one submitted to is Christ.

- A wife cannot be a biblical wife unless she first gives her heart totally to Christ. She has *no* chance of being able to respect a fallible man unless she first respects the infallible Man.

4. For husbands: Love cannot be truly given unless it is first expressed toward Christ.

- A husband cannot love his wife biblically unless he first loves Christ with all his heart. He has *no* chance of being a consistently great husband until the issue of Lordship is settled in his heart.

5. For parents: Obedience and honor on their part is tied to your willingness to orient them toward Christ.

- Again, it goes back to Christ. Instilling a biblical worldview is more than having a bunch of rules; it's about breathing Christ into them through your heart, words, and actions.

Make no mistake; this "Christ is the key" mind-set (or lack thereof) will affect everything in your home:

- fidelity vs. infidelity
- holiness vs. compromise
- debt vs. financial freedom
- selfishness vs. giving hearts
- consumerism vs. contentment
- dissension vs. unity
- fear vs. faith
- sadness vs. joy
- depression vs. hope
- dishonesty vs. integrity

God's will for family life is that He is the center of that life. He desires our families to put Him first corporately. The key is to realize the plan of the enemy is to keep us focused on and distracted by carnal things, which degrades our ability to cultivate godly lives, marriages, and children. Take a minute to dream about the kind of family life described in Scripture. Take Colossians 3:12–13 as another example:

1. Mercifully tender: a family that is tender with one another
2. Kind: without yelling, arguing, grudge holding, etc.
3. Humble and meek: putting others before ourselves
4. Patient: not being so quick to judge or retaliate; willing to wait until God changes a heart
5. Bearing and forgiving: repenting quickly and causing harmony and love to rule our home

I want to challenge you today to "put on" or make a decision to love Christ above all else, and plant His cross in the middle of your family!

The How (Some thoughts from Colossians 3:15–25):

1. Let peace rule your home. Suggestion: Forgive and handle disagreements according to the Word. Live holy.
2. Let the word saturate your home. Suggestion: Institute times of Bible study in your "small group."
3. Let discipleship happen within your home. Suggestion: Encourage each other in holiness, obedience, faith, and purpose.
4. Let worship go forth in your home. Suggestion: Worship the Lord together at home and in church.
5. Let each member operate in his or her role. Suggestion: Commit to living God's way as a spouse, single person, or parent.
6. Let work and service flow out of your home. Suggestion: Serve the kingdom through serving the church with excellence.

Jesus Is Enough Assignment:

1. List five ways you can inject "more of Christ into your daily living.
2. List three ways you can shift more toward Christ and a Christian worldview in your behaviors and thoughts.

3. List three ways or things you can sacrifice for the good of your family.
4. Name the person you can share these with for accountability.

_____
_____
_____
_____
_____
_____
_____
_____

LESSON
30

THE THOUGHT PATTERNS OF
A MATURE CHRISTIAN

Read Ephesians 6:5–20

When I started teaching the book of Ephesians in my church, I said this:

> Is Jesus still enough for you!? We have spent the last few months reframing our perspective on the kingdom of God, what true harvest means, and how to look at the Scriptures. Just reading the Word (instead of reading into it) has allowed us to arrive at an unselfish (and for some an uncomfortable) place, as we've discovered that the kingdom is about Christ taking over the man rather than the Christian taking over the marketplace.
>
> However, I believe our refocus on the core truths of the Word will help us to live and minister *with new levels of power* because we are effectively moving ourselves (our ambitions, our wants, our desires, etc.) out of the way, and inserting the will God. We have starved ourselves of the fast food of what I call "Systematic Blessing Theology," and we are eating healthy meals. We are getting stronger in the faith because we have decided to embrace real Christianity. So, I believe that we can now begin to embrace and execute what this church is truly here for:
>
> 1. To reach, teach, and release hurting people through the power of Jesus Christ.
> 2. To help those same people discover life at Calvary (as it is presented in the Scriptures and not what we want it to be).
> 3. To present to our area and beyond a model of Christian integrity by the way we communicate Scripture, conduct our lives, manage our money, and walk in love with each other.
> 4. To penetrate culture and present Christ in fresh and innovative ways.

5. To fly a standard of biblical fidelity and to equip believers to share their faith.

As we conclude the book, my mission in this lesson is not so much to present an exegesis of the individual pieces of spiritual armor, but rather the overall call to warfare and the worldview they represent. Today, I'd simply like to sound the urgent call of Paul in this book: *to unify all things under Christ!*

Critical Shifts in Perspective: The thought patterns of a mature Christian

1. The purpose of life is Christ (vv. 5–8)

    In order to walk in His power and anointing, everything we do must have His glory as our aim and His glory as our motivation! This is an intentional moving away from a focus on our own purpose to seeking His purpose. This is the worldview we must instill in our children and into every convert. Sadly, the lack of this very basic ideal is why selfishness and sin run rampant–even in Christian families.

2. Succeeding in purpose requires the right posture (vv. 10, 11)

    After giving the church such a great vision, Paul says, "Finally." The context indicates that his next statement is critical to accomplishing all he has taught. Essentially, Paul is saying, "No matter what, do these things." This is the kind of attitude we need to have today. Our attitude should be "no matter what, I will live for Christ." I believe that if we had this kind of attitude, 80 percent of our problems would be addressed and would cause a revival the likes of which we've never seen!

3. The right posture encourages the right perception (v. 12)

    Posture is an important part of understanding the Christian worldview. There are real spiritual forces out to destroy as many people as possible. Instead of yelling at the Devil, we instead perceive the need to:

    1. "Submit [ourselves], therefore, to God. Resist the devil, and he will flee from you. Draw near to God, and he will draw near to you. Cleanse your hands, you sinners, and purify your hearts" (James 4:7–8).
    2. "Be alert and of sober mind because our enemy the devil prowls around like a roaring lion looking for someone to devour." (1 Peter 5:8–9). We will resist him by standing firm in the faith.

We are slowly understanding that screaming at Satan while failing in our prayer lives and personal behavior does very little, and doesn't advance the kingdom cause.

4. This perception drives us toward spiritual preparation (vv. 13–17)

This goes back to item 2. Being fully dressed for battle starts with the right attitude. The right attitude will cause you to:

1. Stand for Christ no matter what (v. 13)
2. Fight against relativism and for the singular truth of Christ (v. 14)
3. Live holy and with a pure heart (v. 14)
4. Share your faith with wisdom and love (v. 15)
5. Trust God no matter what (v. 16)
6. Live with the joy of your unshakeable salvation (v. 17)
7. And be a fervent student and applier of the Word! (v. 17)

5. A daily part of our preparation for battle includes prayer (vv. 18–20).

Please remember that:

1. Prayer is about lining your will up with His, not the other way around.
2. Once that "posture" is established in prayer, trust God!
3. God is looking for sincerity in prayer, not "vain repetitions." (Matt. 6:7)
4. Prayer encourages discipline and God-focus, which is a good thing!
5. Prayer and study go together. Your devotional life increases the quality of life.

Jesus Is Enough Questions: Do you really see the battle raging around us? Do you really understand that the "me first" mind-set of contemporary Christianity will not help us fight this battle? Have you internalized the fact that only when Christ becomes our life can we truly give up that life in His service? Express your feelings below.

_____

_____

_____

_____

_____

_____

_____

_____

_____

_____

_____

_____

_____

FINAL THOUGHTS

If then you have been raised with Christ, seek the things that are above,
where Christ is, seated at the right hand of God. Set your minds on things
that are above, not on things that are on earth. For you have died, and your
life is hidden with Christ in God. When Christ who is your life appears, then
you also will appear with him in glory. Put to death therefore what is earthly
in you: sexual immorality, impurity, passion, evil desire, and covetousness,
which is idolatry. On account of these the wrath of God is coming
(Col. 3:1–6)

I began this book because I wanted to chronicle my journey from a believer and pastor who was confused and a bit disillusioned about ministry to one who is excited about the clarity and purpose that I found in Christ. That journey is summed up in the phrase *Jesus is enough*!

So many precious saints are wandering in their walk with the Lord, trying to find some true peace and true joy in this life. The truth is that those things are not found naturally in this world. True peace and true joy can only be found in Jesus. Oh sure, we can and will have times of wonderful happiness when we get a new job or when a baby is born or when we have a really good time at a get-together. And those things are great. But those aren't the things that gave the apostles the joy and strength to brave lions, be set on fire and to give their lives for Christ. *Jesus is enough* is our way of saying that He alone is worth living for and everything else, no matter how nice, will let you down or be taken from you eventually.

The apostle Peter said it best:

> *Blessed be the God and Father of our Lord Jesus Christ! According to his
> great mercy, he has caused us to be born again to a living hope through
> the resurrection of Jesus Christ from the dead, to an inheritance that is
> imperishable, undefiled, and unfading, kept in heaven for you, who by God's*

power are being guarded through faith for a salvation ready to be revealed in the last time. In this you rejoice, though now for a little while, if necessary, you have been grieved by various trials, so that the tested genuineness of your faith--more precious than gold that perishes though it is tested by fire--may be found to result in praise and glory and honor at the revelation of Jesus Christ.

Though you have not seen him, you love him. Though you do not now see him, you believe in him and rejoice with joy that is inexpressible and filled with glory, obtaining the outcome of your faith, the salvation of your souls. Concerning this salvation, the prophets who prophesied about the grace that was to be yours searched and inquired carefully, inquiring what person or time the Spirit of Christ in them was indicating when he predicted the sufferings of Christ and the subsequent glories. It was revealed to them that they were serving not themselves but you, in the things that have now been announced to you through those who preached the good news to you by the Holy Spirit sent from heaven, things into which angels long to look.

Therefore, preparing your minds for action, and being sober-minded, set your hope fully on the grace that will be brought to you at the revelation of Jesus Christ. As obedient children, do not be conformed to the passions of your former ignorance, but as he who called you is holy, you also be holy in all your conduct, since it is written, "You shall be holy, for I am holy." And if you call on him as Father who judges impartially according to each one's deeds, conduct yourselves with fear throughout the time of your exile, knowing that you were ransomed from the futile ways inherited from your forefathers, not with perishable things such as silver or gold, but with the precious blood of Christ, like that of a lamb without blemish or spot.

He was foreknown before the foundation of the world but was made manifest in the last times for the sake of you who through him are believers in God, who raised him from the dead and gave him glory, so that your faith and hope are in God. Having purified your souls by your obedience to the truth for a sincere brotherly love, love one another earnestly from a pure heart, since you have been born again, not of perishable seed but of imperishable, through the living and abiding word of God; for "All flesh is like grass and all its glory like the flower of grass. The grass withers, and the flower falls, but the word of the Lord remains forever." And this word is the good news that was preached to you. (1 Pet. 1:3–25)

May our Lord and Christ bless you and keep you.
Soli Deo Gloria.

NOTES

Preface

1. John MacArthur, *The Gospel according to Jesus: What is authentic faith?* (Grand Rapids, Mich.: Zondervan, 2008)
2. John MacArthur, *Hard to believe: the high cost and infinite value of following Jesus* (Nashville, Tenn.: Thomas Nelson, 2003)
3. Hank Hanegraaff, *Christianity in Crisis* (Eugene, Oregon: Harvest House, 1993)

Lesson 3: Recommitting to Character

1. Andy Stanley, *Visioneering: Fulfilling God's purpose through intentional living* (Sisters, Oregon: Multnomah, 1999), 190-191

Lesson 15: Christology, Part 2

1. Matt Slick, "Jesus' Two Natures: God and Man." *Christian Apologetics & Research Ministry: http://carm.org/jesus-two-natures* (November 1, 2013)

Lesson 29: The Key to the Home is Christ!

1. Dave Ramsey, "Dave Ramsey's Momentum." *Daveramsey.com.* www.daveramsey.com